PRAY THE HOLY MASS

by Fr. Paul Trinchard, S.T.L.

"Behold the HEAVENLY RAINBOW"
St. Leonard of Port Maurice

"Of all holy things, this SACRIFICE
(as expressed in the Tridentine or Canonized Liturgy)
IS THE MOST HOLY..."

Ch. 4, Dogmatic Council of Trent

MARIAN PUBLICATIONS, INC.
MONROVIA CALIFORNIA

Published by MARIAN PUBLICATIONS, INC.
Printed in the United States of America

Library of Congress Number
94-072-984

ISBN 1-886492-02-6

MARIAN PUBLICATIONS, INC.
PO BOX 232
MONROVIA, CALIFORNIA 91017

"BEHOLD THE HEAVENLY RAINBOW,
pacifying the storms of Divine Justice!
For myself, I believe that
were it not for *the Holy Mass,*
at this present moment
the world would be in the abyss,
unable to bear up
under the mighty load
of its iniquities."

St. Leonard of Port Maurice

COVER PICTURE

Shortly after the Novus Ordo Mass or New Order was imposed on us, two dedicated laymen, along with the help of others, on the high desert of Nevada sixty miles from Reno in Silver Springs, built their own church for the celebration of Christ's Canonized Liturgy of the Latin-Rite Mass. These people withdrew as did John the Baptist and his followers.

They also went out to a desert similar in appearance to the deserts of Israel. Did they not go AS EXILES from the establishment church on behalf of the Real Church, as defined by its binding and God-given "semper et ubique" official orthodoxy and orthopraxis?

During the Mass of consecration for this church by Bishop Williamson, an arch-shaped multi-colored rainbow initially formed in the desert sky. This rainbow-arch dipped down to the church's steeple on one end and on the southern end into the adjacent sun-lit desert.

Then, an even more unusual sight followed. The multi-colored rainbow-arch suddenly turned totally golden and illuminated the church. A real golden arch appeared in the blue desert sky to set apart this recently built church during the hour in which it was being solemnly dedicated to the celebration of the establishment-outlawed Canonized Liturgy of all times.

THIS ENTIRE EVENT WAS CAPTURED ON VIDEO. THE COVER PICTURE (FRONT) IS AN ARTISTIC RENDITION OF THE ACTUAL EVENT. THE BACK COVER FEATURES PHOTOGRAPHS MADE FROM TWO ACTUAL FRAMES OF THIS VIDEO, SHOWING THE TWO ENDS OF THE RAINBOW.

God's Providence didn't stop here. Subsequently, Pope John Paul II personally ordered the bishop of Nevada to supply a Canonized Latin Rite Mass to this people-built and people-owned church.

FORWARD

Must we not perceive THE Canonized Mass as St. Leonard did? Is it not THE HEAVENLY RAINBOW--God's promise and OUR hope for liturgical ecclesial re-Par-ation, or restoration to the PAR?

Can we not read into these spectacular or even miraculous HAPPENINGS (in the Nevada desert) greater significance-- signs for OUR future? Bishop Sheen predicted that laymen will help to bring about the restoration of the Church.

What can YOU do? At least, appreciate, support and PRAY THE HOLY MASS. God assures us that one day a pope will fully OBEY GOD'S FATIMA COMMANDS. In doing so, this pope will bring about full ecclesial reparation.

Better appreciate THE HOLY MASS which has been stolen from you. The future success of those who strive to re-par or restore the Church is assured. Their desert or catacomb efforts will be blessed by God even though their present success--as measured by buildings and people--will for some time be minimal.

READ THIS BOOK CAREFULLY. PRAY THIS BOOK OFTEN. THEN YOU'LL BE MORE DEDICATED TO ECCLESIAL RE-PARATION.

The dedicated Liturgical Remnant constitutes a significant part of THE HOPE for our future. This book of meditations and prayers is written to help this dedicated remnant and their converts to better PRAY THE CANONIZED CATHOLIC MASS or THE HOLY MASS of the Catholic Latin Rite.

Even NOW, do not THE HOLY MASSES of which St. Leonard speaks "pacify the storms of Divine Justice?" Reading, meditating and praying "from" this book will help you to PRAY THE perpetually Canonized HOLY MASS.

DEDICATION and THANKS

This book is dedicated to the very few bishops, priests and the few laymen who support and promote the HOLY Mass-- that Mass which Pope Saint Pius V CANONIZED and which Pope Saint Pius X urged us TO PRAY when he said: "PRAY THE HOLY MASS."

Indeed, we implore the help of these saints, the only canonized popes of the Modern Era, as we pray and work that this Mass--which they LOVED and which sanctified them and countless others--may be fully restored to its proper place within the Existential Catholic Church.

In a special way, this book is dedicated to the living and deceased who built and/or now support the "CL" or "Canonized-Liturgy" Church in Silver Springs, Nevada, as explained on the back cover.

My thanks are extended to those many "conservatives" who brought me back to the true and full Catholic Faith by boldly and persistently witnessing to it.

For those who labored to help with this book, I thank Phyllis Schabow and Vera Muller.

My special thanks to my largest financial supporter and friend, Richard Ahearn, for his contributions. I pray that others may be inspired to imitate his generosity in donating to MARIAN PUBLICATIONS for similar future works.

"Go, show yourselves as my beloved children:

I am with you and in you, provided that your faith
be the light that enlightens you in these days of woe.
May your zeal cause you to be as famished
for the glory and honor of Jesus Christ.

Fight, children of light, you
LITTLE NUMBER WHO SEE CLEARLY.
For behold, the time of times,
the end of ends."

The Secret of La Salette
The Blessed Virgin to Melanie

A WORD OF ADVICE TO THOSE WHO ARE COMING

FROM THE NEW AND NOVEL INTO THE OLD AND PERENNIAL

Many readers of this "prayer book"--especially, young ones--have already been indoctrinated into NOEL (the Novus Ordo English Liturgy) as it exists now and as it is devolving. Be patient "with yourself."

It will take some time for you to get used to the truly and substantially serious. As you do, you'll come to perceive NOEL--the Novus Ordo English Liturgy--as being hypocritical or false; and, superficial or sense-oriented.

NOEL (Novus Ordo English Liturgy) is engineered to be performed as a man-oriented pleasantly LYING LITURGY. Its major lie is: MAN IS AS GOD. The goal of the Novus Ordo English Liturgy (NOEL) is to make each of its VICTIMS FEEL good about their NOEL-assured God-hood.

God has blessed you with this "prayer book." Be patient "with yourself." Be grateful to God.

God has led you to be able to COMPARE the two opposing and contradictory LITURGIES. Yes, these two liturgies oppose each other. The leaders of NOEL (Novus Ordo English Liturgy) admit this by what they say and do. This is cogently evident from even a casual study of the edicts emanating from NOEL's bishops.

The Canonized Liturgy (CL) is treated as INTOLERABLE. At most, CL is allowed a "token" existence. Why? NOEL (Novus Ordo English Liturgy) has been seen for what it is--alien and contradictory to the Canonized Liturgy (CL). Two opposing liturgies vie for YOUR allegiance.

It took many months of celebrating CL or the Canonized Liturgy, for me to see the truth about the Novus Ordo English

Liturgy (NOEL). Compare. Comparison proved!

Let me give a few examples of what I saw and what you will see. I started celebrating CL--the Canonized Liturgy--after twenty-six years of "celebrating" NOEL--the Novus Ordo English Liturgy, i.e. around 1992.

I first perceived that the Canonized Liturgy, (CL) was GOD directed and NOT "MAN-AS-GOD" directed. I alone celebrated MASS. No longer was I the M.C. or showmaster for the precious community's "celebration."

Indeed, NOEL--the Novus Ordo English Liturgy--implied and effectively taught homology (MAN-centered-ness) together with its presently popular HERESIES. CL--the Canonized Liturgy--came from, prayed and thus re-taught the saving-truths of the Real Catholic Church.

CL (Canonized Liturgy) led people away from heresies. NOEL (Novus Ordo English Liturgy) at least subtly leads its victims into heresies.

CHRIST was offered to God for our sins. The Novus Ordo English Liturgy (NOEL) conveys the impression that it offers mere bread and wine (no wonder some NOEL presiders want to add pretzels and beer). NOEL in a fake and shallow way also had offertory processions where NOEL pretended to offer to God, especially for the kiddies, all kinds of THINGS-- from books to pussy cats.

THE PRIEST in CL (Canonized Liturgy) prays "the offering of Christ" FOR our salvation and sanctification; AND, FOR the souls in Purgatory. Being ordained for CL, which I didn't say until 1992, I was ORDAINED to offer the sacrifice of the MASS for the LIVING and DEAD, the souls in Purgatory. I wasn't ordained TO RECEIVE the community's gifts, whatever that might mean and for whatever that might be worth.

The Novus Ordo English Liturgy (NOEL) celebrates each

one's goodness as it prays for "MORE GOODIES"-- goodies from a safe holiday season to the conquest of prejudice by love and mercy, whatever this might mean. The Canonized Liturgy (CL) focuses on SALVATION, SANCTIFICATION AND RELEASE FROM PURGATORY.

The Canonized Liturgy (CL) clearly has THE PRIEST as sole celebrant who celebrates the Unbloody Sacrifice of Calvary IN PERSONA CHRISTI. CL's mandated gestures and prayers "force" the priest to be Christ. He, THE PRIEST, is forced to ACT IN PERSONA CHRISTI by the very prayers and gestures of the ritual.

NOEL (Novus Ordo English Liturgy) leads the priest to be an MC who MERELY NARRATES what happened at the Last Supper. The showmaster recalls that other great "sacramental and signed" (two of their presently favored politically correct words) supper at a protestant-like table preferably separated from God in His tabernacle.

The Canonized Liturgy (CL) re-does THE SACRIFICE or THE SAVING-ACT. CL brings each INTO Heaven as it brings to us "the Lamb AS slain." Therefore, those who attend MASS are either merely "present to" the MASS or "IN" the Mass, as the pre-ordained elect for whom the Saving-Act saves. That's why, if at all possible, CL has Mass before God in His tabernacle.

For the Novus Ordo English Liturgy (NOEL), the Mass is becoming more and more "a" or "the" SACRAMENT AND SIGN of each man's salvation. Therefore, "For ALL" as understood by Americans, along with other liturgical confessions of universal salvation ABOUND WITHIN NOEL. NOEL teaches heresy.

How successful is NOEL's liturgy? NOEL--the Novus Ordo English Liturgy--implies or effectively teaches UNIVERSAL SALVATION. Well over sixty percent of NOEL's "priests" don't believe in transubstantiation. Over eighty percent of NOEL's VICTIMS, (those under fifty years of age) REJECT THE CATHOLIC DOGMA ON THE EUCHARIST.

Indeed, THE Sacrament flows from THE Sacrifice. As sacrifice is denied, the sacrament is denied and "sacrileged."

As you go into CL's liturgy, you'll notice that Catholics relate to the Eucharist as Christ who is NOW present "to" that which appears to be bread. Each particle of that which appears to be bread IS Christ--Body, Blood, Soul and Divinity. Each such "particle" is Adorable, and is treated as being Adorable.

On the other hand, NOEL treats the "Holy Bread" as bread. Since NOEL no longer REALLY believes in "Christ's Eucharistic Presence," it allows or even mandates reception in the hand. NOEL also commands each of its eucharistic ministers to refer to the person or to the community (and NOT the Sacred Host) as she/he says "Body (or Blood) of Christ."

Each is Christ in NOEL's homology. The Eucharist then becomes "sign and sacrament" of each one's "Christ-ness."

I have only given you a FEW insights. Let the Holy Ghost enlighten you from truth to truth as you read and pray. Let God--in His own timing--remove your evil and prejudiced "convictions."

Be patient. Be grateful. Prayerfully attending CL will bring you to a more prayerful understanding of the only canonized and classical Mass of the Latin Rite of the Roman Catholic Church.

Don't fear the truth--the truth about NOEL (Novus Ordo English Liturgy) and CL (Canonized Liturgy). Let CL lead you--by grace and inspiration--back into the fullness and clarity of Catholic liturgy and belief.

As far back as 1861, Cardinal Manning saw very clearly that the CESSATION OF THE HOLY MASS was coming, having read carefully the writings of the Fathers on this subject from the earliest times. This great Cardinal gives us the following inspired predictions:

"The Holy Fathers who have written upon the subject of Anti-Christ, and of the prophecies of Daniel, WITHOUT A SINGLE EXCEPTION, as far as I know--and they are the Fathers both of the East and of the West, the Greek and the Latin Church--all of them unanimously--say that in the latter end of the world, during the reign of Antichrist, THE HOLY SACRIFICE OF THE ALTAR WILL CEASE. In the work on the end of the world, ascribed to St. Hippolytus, after a long description of the afflictions of the last days, we read as follows:

"The Churches shall lament with a great lamentation, for THERE SHALL BE OFFERED NO MORE OBLATION NOR WORSHIP ACCEPTABLE TO GOD. The sacred buildings of the churches shall be as hovels; and the precious Body and Blood of Christ shall NOT be manifest in those days; the True Liturgy shall become extinct...Such is the UNIVERSAL TESTIMONY of the Fathers of the early centuries.'"

CRISIS OF THE HOLY SEE
1861

DEFINITIONS

CL--the Canonized Liturgy, which was canonized by Apostolic Tradition, the "Sensus Fidelium," the Council of Trent and Pope St. Pius V.

ESSENTIAL CHURCH--the church as it should be, or the real Church as composed of all truly Catholic believers. This Church may only be numbered in the thousands IN OUR DAY. This Church is THE REMNANT. Usually, when I refer to "essential church," I am referring to the church as it should be BUT ACTUALLY ISN'T.

EXISTENTIAL CHURCH--the church as it exists. As such, (because it is made up of human beings) it can be in apostasy and be wicked--in part or even nearly totally. Usually, when I refer to "existential church," I am referring to the church as it actually exists AND as it SHOULDN'T EVER EXIST.

HOMOLOGY--in contrast to theology, which is God-centered, homology is MAN-centered.

NAC--New Age Catholicism which is Man-centered; and dethrones God; and rejects or modifies God's Revelations.

NOEL--The Novus Ordo English Liturgy as it exists--by imposition or as tolerated.

A NOTE FOR ALL READERS--
ESPECIALLY CRITICAL ONES

I am a Catholic theologian. As such, I demand (but really don't expect to receive) the same privileges that famous American (heretical--at least, by what they IMPLY) scholars or theologians enjoy. I demand that I not be persecuted for stating or implying my UNPOPULAR and NOT "locally" and presently POLITICALLY CORRECT Traditional CATHOLIC BELIEFS. I demand a "theologian's immunity" for being a true Catholic.

Obviously--as Cardinal Ratzinger implied by his endorsement of Msgr. Klaus Gamber's bold and harsh criticism of the Novus Ordo (in THE REFORM OF THE ROMAN LITURGY) the Novus Ordo and, a fortiori, the Novus Ordo English Liturgy (NOEL) COMPRISE (as Cardinal Ratzinger's predecessor, Cardinal Ottaviani, stated) AN ALIEN RELIGION.

The pain that NOEL-indoctrinated victims feel or experience in reading this prayer-book comes from the REALIZATION THAT THEIR NOEL-RELIGION IS IN CONFLICT WITH "THAT OTHER RELIGION"--TRUE CATHOLICISM. I urge such victims not to let this pain destroy them. Instead, turn this pain into gain.

The conflict of religions becomes "clearer and more convincing" as one properly prays THE Holy Mass--the Canonized Liturgy (CL) of the Latin Rite of the Catholic Church. If you are a NOEL-victim, let your PAIN be resolved to your GAIN. Embrace the truth and be positive to God and to His Church's religion, and be negative to any "alien religion."

For your own good--don't attack the Canonized Liturgy of the Catholic Church. Instead, be POSITIVE to that which appears to be (from your NOEL-indoctrinations or NOEL-victimhood) "the liturgy of that other essentially different religion." For your own eternal good--BE POSITIVE TO THE CANONIZED CATHOLIC LITURGY.

If you are a priest, pray the Canonized Liturgy. Such is your RIGHT as given in a fully and binding fashion by: Apostolic Tradition; the Sensus Fidelium as liturgized; Church usage for over 1900 years; Dogmatic Councils, especially those of Florence and Trent; and, the fully binding "eternal" decrees of one of the only two pope-saints of modern times, Pope St. Pius V. The other pope-saint, Pope St. Pius X, endorsed Pope St. Pius V by commanding: "PRAY THE HOLY MASS."

If you are a priest, let this book entice you to discover or re-discover what it REALLY MEANS TO BE CHRIST'S PRIEST. PRAY the Holy Mass; pray the Canonized Liturgy which you as a priest have a perfect RIGHT to pray.

If you are a layman, let this book help you to obey Pope St. Pius X by praying, as best you can, that Mass--the Canonized Liturgy--which he commanded us to pray: "PRAY THE HOLY MASS." PRAY THE CANONIZED LITURGY whenever you can.

This is the Mass that made many of our spiritual ancestors into saints, by bringing them into Heaven. Let it do the same for YOU. Be POSITIVE, not negative, TO THE HOLY MASS, the Canonized Mass of our Catholic Church.

BE EDIFIED OR BE SANCTIFIED through PRAYING THE HOLY MASS. May this book help you to do this.

ST. ROBERT BELLARMINE

ST. ROBERT BELLARMINE was a great theologian.
He taught that anyone who attacked the
Catholic Faith must be resisted with all
the ability that God has granted us.
He did not hesitate to tell Catholics
that they must even resist
misguided clergy of any level.

O ST. ROBERT BELLARMINE,
through the intercession
of Our Lady of Fatima,
who chose to exalt your feast day
by appearing on May 13th,
help our Holy Father, our cardinals,
our bishops, our priests and ourselves
to always put loyalty to our Catholic Faith
above all human loyalties.

THE FATIMA CRUSADER

TABLE OF CONTENTS

PART ONE
DISCOVERING OR BETTER UNDERSTANDING THE HOLY MASS

PART TWO
PRAY THE HOLY MASS

CHAPTER SEVEN

PART THREE
PRAYERS AND MEDITATIONS

CHAPTER EIGHT

CHAPTER NINE

CHAPTER TEN

CHAPTER ELEVEN

"Novelty is a sure mark of heresy."
St Vincent of Lerins

"Any innovation in matters of Faith is
extremely pernicious and utterly damnable!"

St John Eudes

"Innovators must daily seek after something new,
and newer still and are always longing to add something
to religion, or to change it or to subtract from it."

St. Vincent of Lerins

PART ONE

DISCOVERING OR BETTER APPRECIATING

THE HOLY MASS

PRAY THE HOLY MASS

"Don't pray AT Holy Mass, but PRAY THE HOLY MASS...
the highest prayer that exists...

You have to associate your heart with the holy feelings
which are contained in THE PRIEST'S words,

and in this manner you ought to follow
all that happens on the Altar.

When acting in this way
you have PRAYED THE HOLY MASS."

His Holiness POPE SAINT PIUS X

THE HIDDEN TREASURE
by St. Leonard of Port Maurice
is the basis for my comments
in Chapters One and Two.

It has been quoted
with permission of
TAN BOOKS AND PUBLISHERS, INC.

THE HIDDEN TREASURE
is still available @ $4.00 from

TAN BOOKS AND PUBLISHERS, INC.
PO BOX 424
ROCKFORD, ILLINOIS 61105

CHAPTER ONE

THE HOLY MASS FULFILLS YOUR BASIC OBLIGATIONS TO GOD

St. Thomas (Summa Theologica, 1, ii., art.3) spells out the ways in which we must know, love and "minister to" God. First of all, we must praise and honor God's infinite Majesty. Such is most worthy of infinite honor and praise. WE MUST ADORE GOD.

Secondly, we must satisfy for so many sins committed against that infinite Majesty. WE MUST OBTAIN REPARATION FOR OUR OWN SINS.

The third is to thank Him for so many benefits received. WE MUST THANK GOD.

The fourth is to supplicate Him as the Giver of all graces. WE MUST BE CHARITABLE. WE MUST PETITION GOD FOR OTHERS.

How shall we wretched creatures, who are in a state of dependence for the very breath we draw, ever be able to fulfill TIIESE PRIMARY ORLIGATIONS? Let us attend or celebrate (if one is a priest) as many Masses as we can, with all possible devotion, and to have many Masses said for ourselves, "ours," and the departed. More specifically, we now inquire as to HOW Masses fulfill our fourfold obligation to God.

I. WE MUST ADORE GOD

The first obligation by which we are bound toward God is to adore Him. It is indeed a precept of the natural law itself that every inferior owes homage to his superior, and the higher the superiority, so much the deeper the homage that should be offered. Since Almighty God possesses a greatness utterly unbounded, there is due to Him an unbounded honor.

I am a wretched sinner. Where shall I ever find an offering worthy of my Creator? Turn your eyes round among all the creatures of the universe--no, you will not find one that is worthy of God. Ah, no! An offering worthy of God can be none other than God Himself!

God needs descend to lay Himself a Victim on our altars, in order that the homage rendered may perfectly correspond to the eminence of that infinite Majesty. This is effected in holy Mass. In it Almighty God is honored as He deserves, because He is honored by (as) God Himself, that is to say, by Jesus, Who, placing Himself Victim on the altar, with an act of inexplicable submission, adores the Most Holy Trinity, even as "IT" is adorable--in such manner that all other acts of homage, by all other beings, vanish before the face of this self-humiliation of Jesus, as candles before the sun.

It is told of a holy soul that, enamored of God, the fire of her charity flashed forth in a thousand longings. "O my God," she said, "my God, would that I had as many hearts, as many tongues as there are leaves on the trees, atoms of the air, and drops in the waters, that I might so love Thee, and so honor Thee, as Thou deservest! Oh, had I but in this hand all creatures, I would place them at Thy feet, so that all might melt themselves away in love before Thee; and then, oh, that I might love Thee more than all of them united--yes, more than all the angels, more than all the saints, more than all paradise itself!"

One day when she had prayed this with the utmost fervor, she heard herself thus answered by Our Lord: "Console, yourself, my daughter; one Mass heard with devotion will render to Me all that glory which you desire and infinitely more."

Our good Jesus, being not only man, but omnipotent God, by humiliating Himself on the altar, offers in that act of humiliation to the Most Holy Trinity homage and honor infinite; so that we who join with Him in offering the great sacrifice--we through Him--render an infinite homage and honor unto God. Oh, how great a Reality!

By attending holy Mass, we can render to God homage and honor infinite. A soul assisting with adequate devotion at holy Mass renders more honor to God than that which all the angels and all the saints put together render with all their adorations done apart from the Mass. For, after all, they also are but mere creatures, and their homage is therefore limited and finite; whereas, in Mass, Jesus humbles Himself, a humiliation of infinite merit and value; and thus the homage and honor which we through Him give to God in Mass is an infinite homage and honor.

II. WE MUST OBTAIN REPARATION FOR OUR SINS

The second obligation by which we are bound toward God is to satisfy His justice for our many sins. Oh, what a measureless debt is this! One single mortal sin so weighs in the scales of divine justice, that to satisfy for it, all the good works of all the martyrs and of all the saints who as yet have existed, who exist now, or ever shall exist, by or in itself would not suffice.

However, by the holy sacrifice of the Mass, viewed according to its intrinsic preciousness and value, satisfaction may be completely made for all committed sin. Although Jesus is the very party offended, yet, not content with having satisfied divine justiice for us on Calvary, He has bestowed, and continuously bestows, on us this method of satisfaction in the holy sacrifice of Mass.

In the Mass, Jesus renews His offering already made on the Cross to the Eternal Father for the sins of the whole world. That same divine blood which was once paid down as the general ransom of the whole human race comes to be specially applied to each of us individually, as it is offered in Mass for the sins of THE PRIEST who celebrates, and of all those who devoutly attend such a holy sacrifice.

Subjectively considered, the sacrifice of Mass does not cancel our sins immediately and of itself, as does the Sacrament of Penance: but it cancels them mediately, calling down various aids of interior impulse, of holy aspiration, and of actual grace, all tending toward a worthy repentance of our sins, either at the time of Mass itself or at some other fitting time.

God alone knows how many souls issue from the filth of sins through the extraordinary aids which come to them by this divine sacrifice. Indeed the man in mortal sin is not aided by the sacrifice as a propitiation, yet it avails as supplication; and therefore even those in mortal sin ought to hear many Masses, in order to obtain more easily the grace of conversion.

However, those who live in grace "by their Masses" maintain that happy or sanctified state. Also, for such just souls, each Mass cancels (according to the most common view) the guilt of venial sins, provided, at least, that as a whole these sins are repented (of), according to what St. Augustine clearly says: "He who devoutly hears holy Mass will receive a great vigor to enable him to resist mortal sin, and there shall be pardoned to him venial sins which he may have committed up to that hour." O blessed Mass, setting at liberty the sons of God, and satisfying all the penalties due to so many offences!

You will perhaps think that it suffices to hear only one single Mass to strike off the heaviest debts due to God through many committed sins, because, Mass being of infinite value, we can therewith pay to God an infinite satisfaction. Indeed, Mass is of infinite value. You must know, nevertheless, that Almighty God accepts it in a manner limited and finite, and in degrees conformable to the greater or lesser perfection in the dispositions of THE PRIEST who celebrates or the layman who devoutly attends THE sacrifice.

"Quorum tibi fides cognita est, et nota devotio," says holy Church, in the Canon of Mass. This canonized phrase suggests that which the great teachers expressly lay down; namely, that the greater or lesser satisfaction applied in our behalf by the sacrifice becomes determined by the higher or lower dispositions of THE PRIEST who celebrates or of each one who attends Mass as mentioned.

Now, what about the spiritual attitude of those who go in search of the quickest and least devoutly conducted Masses, and what is worse, attend them with little or no devotion; or who have little zeal in selecting more fervent and devout priests. According to St. Thomas, all the Holy Sacrifices are, as sacraments, equal in rank; but they are not, therefore, equal in the effects resulting from them. The greater the actual or habitual piety of THE PRIEST, so much the greater will be the fruit of the application of the Mass; so that not to recognize the diffcrence between a tepid and devout priest, in respect to the efficacy of his Mass, will be simply not to heed whether the net with which you fish is small or great. This also applies in regard to those attending Mass.

Therefore, attend many Masses, yet have far more regard to devotion in hearing the Mass than to the number heard. If you have more devotion in one single Mass than another man in fifty, you will give more honor to God in that single Mass. You will extract greater fruit from it in the way called ex opere operato, than that other with all his fifty.

Through one single Mass, attended with singularly perfect devotion, it might possibly happen that the justice of God would allow the satisfaction for all the transgressions of some great sinner. This is quite in harmony with what the holy Council of Trent teaches; namely, that by the holy sacrifice of the Mass, God grants the gift of penitence. By means of true penitence He pardons the most grave and enormous sins. Yet notwithstanding all this, since neither the internal dispositions with which you attend Mass are manifest to yourself, nor the amount of satisfaction which you receive is known to you, you should do all in your power to attend many Masses and to attend each Mass with as much devotion as possible.

Maintain a great confidence in the living mercy of God, which shines so wonderfully forth in this divine sacrifice; and with lively faith and devout recollection attend as many Masses as you can. In doing this with perseverance, you may hope to reach heaven without any intervening share in purgatory. To Mass, then, dearest friends, and never allow yourselves to utter the thought, "A Mass more or less is of little consequence."

III. WE MUST THANK GOD

The third obligation which you have TO GOD is that of gratitude for the immense benefits which He bestowed upon us. Consider all the gifts, all the graces you have received from God. Every true gift comes through the very life of Jesus, and His death suffered for us, which immeasurably swells the great debt which we owe to God.

How shall we ever be able sufficiently to thank Him? The law of gratitude is observed by mere animals who sometimes change their cruel anger into gentle homage to their benefactors; and how much more, of course, has it not to be observed by man, gifted as he is with reason.

However, our poverty is so great that there is no way of truly making any return for all the blessings of God; because the least of them all, coming as it does from the hands of majesty so divine, and accompanied as it is by an infinite love on His part, thus acquires an infinite value, and imposes on us a debt of infinite correspondence in the way of reverence and love. O poor, miserable things that we are!

If we are incapable of sustaining the weight of one single benefit, how shall we ever be able to bear the burden of so many, so countlessly many? Must we live and die as it were, ungrateful to our Supreme Benefactor?

Don't "despair." The way most fully to thank our good God was predicted by holy David, who was led by divine inspiration to speak with mysterious reference to this divine sacrifice. He indicated that nothing can sufficiently render the thanks which are due to God, except holy Mass.

Quid retribuam Domino pro omnibus quae retribuit mihi? "What return shall I offer to the Lord for all the benefits which He hath bestowed upon me?" Answering himself, David says, Calicem salutaris accipiam; or Calicem levabo-- "I will uplift on high the chalice of the Lord;" that is, I will offer a sacrifice most grateful to Him, and with this alone I shall satisfy the debt of so many benefits.

The sacrifice of the Mass was instituted by Our Redeemer principally in recognition of the divine beneficence, and as thanks to Him. Therefore it bears as its most special and worthy name the Eucharist, which signifies an Offering of Thanks. He Himself also gave us the example when, in the Last Supper, before the act of consecration in that first Mass, He raised His eyes to heaven and gave thanks to His heavenly Father: Elevatis oculis in caelum, Tibi gratias agens fregit....

O divine thanksgiving, disclosing the chief end for which was instituted this tremendous sacrifice, and which invites us to conform ourselves to the example of our Head, so that in every Mass at which we assist we may know how to avail ourselves of so great a treasure, and offer it in gratitude to our Supreme Benefactor!

The Holy Mass calls down all spiritual graces:

all the goods appertaining to the soul--
repentance for sins, victory over temptations

whether from external trials such as
bad companions and infernal spirits,

or internal...
those arising from rebellious appetites.

The Holy Mass calls down the aid of grace,

so necessary for enabling us to rise up,
to stand upon our feet,
to walk forward in the ways of God.

It calls down many good and holy inspirations
and many internal impulses,

which dispose us to shake off tepidity
and spurs us on to work our best
with greater fervor, with will more prompt,
with intention more upright and pure;

and these bring with them
an inestimable treasure,
being the most effectual means
for obtaining from God

the grace of final perseverance,
on which depends our eternal salvation.

St. Leonard of Port Maurice
TAN PUBLISHERS

I NEED THE MASS

Try to realize how great are your miseries of soul and the need, therefore, that you have of recourse to God; so that at every moment He may assist you. He alone is the beginning, the "sustainer" and the end of every good. You are a SINNER whose only hope of salvation is the Holy Mass.

Jesus, sacrificing Himself, is THE pacifying Victim, THE supplicatory sacrifice, for obtaining from the Father everything of which you have authentic need. In Holy Mass our dear beloved Jesus as the chief and supreme Priest, recommends your cause to the Father, prays for you and makes Himself your advocate.

Also realize that the great and blessed Virgin unites herself with us in prayer to the Eternal Father to obtain for us the graces we need. What confidence should we not conceive of being heard?

What hope, then, what confidence should we not have, knowing that in Mass Jesus Himself prays for us, offers His most Precious Blood to the Eternal Father for us, and makes Himself our advocate! O blessed Mass! O Eucharist Divine!

What graces, virtues and gifts holy Mass calls down! It calls down all spiritual graces, all the goods appertaining to the soul, such as repentance for sins and victory over temptations, whether such result from external trials, as bad companions and infernal spirits, or internal, as for instance, those arising from rebellious appetites. It calls down the aid of grace, so necessary for enabling us to rise up, to stand upon our feet, to walk forward in the ways of God.

It calls down many good and holy inspirations and many internal impulses, which dispose us to shake off tepidity and spurs us on to work our best with greater fervor, with will more prompt, with intention more upright and pure; and these, again, bring with them an inestimable treasure, being the most effectual means for obtaining from God the grace of final perseverance, on which depends our eternal salvation, and the grace of as much moral certainty of eternal bliss as is ever permitted here below.

But further still, each Mass calls down temporal blessings, only in as much as these do not oppose the salvation of the soul, such as health, abundance, peace, with the exclusion of evils which are their opposites, such as pestilences, earthquakes, wars, famines, persecutions, hatreds, calumnies, injuries; in fine, here may we find liberation from all evils which may impede or block our salvation; here may we find enrichment by every sort of benefit, which works for our eternal good.

In a word, holy Mass is the golden key of paradise. In every Mass ask God to make you a great saint--a great saint. Does this seem too much? It is not too much.

O blessed Mass! Expand yet more and more your heart and ask great things of Him, with faith's conviction that you ask of a God Who does not grow poor by giving and therefore, the more you petition the more you will obtain.

Besides the benefits which we ask in holy Mass, our good God grants many others which we do not ask. St. Jerome distinctly declares: "Without doubt, the Lord grants all the favors which are asked of Him in Mass, provided they be those fitting for us; and, which is a matter of greater wonder, ofttimes He grants that also which is not demanded of Him, if we, on our part, put no obstacle in the way."

A famous legend was told by St. Antoninus of two youths, both libertines, who went one day into the forest, one of them having heard Mass, the other not. Soon, it is said, there arose a furious tempest and they heard, amid thunder and lightning, a voice which cried "Slay!" and instantly came a flash which reduced to ashes the one who had not heard Mass. The other, all terrified, was seeking escape, when he heard anew the same voice, which repeated "Slay!" The poor youth expected instant death, when he heard another voice, which answered, "I cannot, I cannot; today he heard, Verbum caro factum est. This Mass will not let me strike."

Oh, how many times hath God freed you from death, or at least from many most grievous perils, through the Mass which you have attended! St. Gregory assures us of this in the fourth of his dialogues: "It is most true that he who attends holy Mass shall be freed from many evils and from many dangers, both foreseen and unforeseen."

"He shall," as St. Augustine sums it up, "be freed from sudden and unprovided death, which is the most terrible stroke launched by Divine Justice against sinners. In order to obtain a wonderful preservative against such a death: attend holy Mass every day, and attend it with all possible devotion."

O unbounded riches of holy Mass! Grasp well this truth: it is possible for you to gain more favor with God by attending or celebrating one single Mass, considered in itself and in its intrinsic worth, than by opening the treasury of your wealth and distributing the whole to the poor, or by going as pilgrim over the whole world and visiting with utmost devotion the sanctuaries of Rome, of Compostella, of Loreto, Jerusalem and the rest. St. Thomas assures us that in Mass are contained all the fruits, all the graces, yea, all those immense treasures which the Son of God poured out so abundantly upon the Church, His Spouse, in the one and only bloody sacrifice of the cross. Each Mass is Calvary repeated on your behalf.

Now, pause a little. Ponder what has been written. Will you again have a difficulty in believing that one single Mass, with its intrinsic worth and value, has such efficacy as to suffice to obtain even the salvation of the whole human race?

Imagine the case that Our Lord Jesus Christ had not suffered anything on Calvary and, in place of His bloody sacrifice of the cross, had solely instituted Mass for our redemption, with an express command that in all the world it should only be celebrated once. Well, then, had this been the case, that single Mass, celebrated by the poorest priest in the world, would have been sufficient, considered in itself and so far as its own share in the work is concerned, to win from God the salvation of all men.

One single Mass, presuming what's been stated, might thus have been made to obtain the conversion of all heretics, all schismatics, all unbelievers, and also that of all bad Christians; closing the gates of Hell to all sinners, and emptying purgatory of all the souls there obtaining purification.

Through our sins, through our tepidity, through our little devotion, and possibly even through our scandalous improprieties we limit and render ineffective the unlimited and almighty work of each Mass we attend or fail to attend.

Why run you not to the churches, there to listen with holy hearts to all the Masses in your power? Why not imitate the holy angels, who, according to St. Chrysostom, when holy Mass is being celebrated, descend and stand before our altars, covered with the wings of reverential awe, waiting the whole of that blessed time, in order that they may intercede for us the more effectively since this is the most opportune time for obtaining favors from heaven. At least, never again even think: "A Mass more or less is of little importance."

IV. WE MUST BE CHARITABLE

WE MUST BE CHARITABLE. WE MUST PETITION GOD FOR HIS GRACE AND MERCY TOWARDS OTHERS--ESPECIALLY THE "POOR" SOULS IN PURGATORY.

One Mass alone, in its own intrinsic value, is sufficient to empty purgatory of all the souls in process of purification, and place them in holy paradise. This divine sacrifice not only avails for the souls of the dead, as propitiatory and satisfactory of their penance, but it also assists as a great act of supplication for them, conformably to the custom of the Church, which not only offers Mass for the souls that are being purified, but prays during the sacrifice for their liberation.

In order, then, that you may be stirred to compassion for the "poor" souls in Purgatory, know that the fire by which they are covered is one so devouring that, according to the opinion of St. Gregory, it is no less than that of hell (Dial. 1. 4, c. 131), operating as the instrument of divine justice with such force as to render their pains greater than all the possible martyrdoms that can be witnessed or felt, or even imagined, here below. Still more than all this, the pain of loss afflicts them because, deprived as they are of the beatific vision of God, they, as the Angelic Doctor says, experience an intolerable passion, an intense and vivid desire to behold the Supreme Good, and this is not yet permitted to them.

If you should see your father or your mother on the point of being drowned, and if to save them would not cost you more than the stretching out of your hand, would not you feel bound by every law of charity and of justice to extend that hand to aid them? How then can you behold with the eyes of faith so many poor souls, and perhaps your nearest and dearest, in a lake of flame, and not endure a little inconvenience in order to attend Masses devoutly, for their sake?

What sort of heart is yours? Do not doubt that holy Mass not only shortens their pains, but also extends great immediate relief to these poor souls. It has even been thought by some that while Mass is being celebrated for a soul, the fire, otherwise most devouring, suspends its rigor, and no pain is suffered by that soul during all the time that the holy sacrifice proceeds. We may well believe, at least, that at every Mass many issue forth from purgatory and fly to holy paradise.

Add this consideration, that the charity which you exercise toward poor souls under purification will all redound to your own good. Examples without end might be adduced in confirmation of this truth, but two will suffice for now.

St. Peter Damian, when left an orphan by his parents, at a tender age, was placed in the house of one of his brothers, who treated him poorly. He was made to go barefoot and in rags, causing him to endure in every way extreme sufferings. One day he happened to find a coin which was a lot of money to him--but how to spend it? His necessities suggested many ways, but instead he decided to give it to a priest that he might celebrate Mass for the Poor Souls in Purgatory. From that time forward, his fortune changed.

He was taken home by another brother who loved him as his son, clothed him with propriety and sent him to school, whence he finally came forth a great saint. Now you see how from one single Mass, obtained at a slight personal inconvenience, all this happiness originated. O blessed Mass, at once assisting the living and the dead, beneficial for time and for eternity!

Realize that the holy souls are so grateful to their benefactors that, once in heaven they become themselves their advocates, nor will they ever rest till they see them in paradise.

It would seem that an unworthy woman in Rome experienced this. Utterly forgetful of her eternal salvation, she had no other heed than to give vent to evil passions, and to ruin her youth. She did little good except that every few days she would get a Mass said for souls in purgatory.

It was they, as we may well believe, who so interceded for their benefactress that one day she was overtaken by vehement contrition for her sins. Abandoning her infamous dwelling, she sped to the feet of a zealous confessor, made her general confession, and soon after died in such good dispositions that she afforded to one and all clear signs of eternal salvation.

This grace so altogether miraculous was generally attributed to the virtue of those Masses celebrated at her request, in behalf of the blessed souls in purgatory. Let us then go and do likewise.

When asked on his death-bed what he had most at heart, and what kindness he most longed for after death, St. John of Avila answered: "Masses, Masses." I should wish in this matter to offer you an advice of great importance. It is this: to procure that all the Masses which you would like to have celebrated for you after death shall be celebrated for you during life. Don't trust to those who remain after you on the scene of this world.

St. Anselm declared that one single Mass heard or celebrated for your soul during life may perhaps be more profitable to you than many after death. Having thoroughly pondered the excellence of holy Mass, wonder at the blindness in which you have lived till now, having formed no right estimate of a treasure which has for you too much remained, as it were, hidden and buried; or insufficiently appreciated.

Now therefore, banish from your mind, the thought that " a Mass more or less matters little;" or "that it is a small thing to hear Mass" or "that the Mass of this or that priest is like a Mass of Holy Week for length; when he appears at the altar it is high time to get out of church." Renew your holy resolution to hear from this time forward as many Masses as you possibly can, and above all, with the greatest possible devotion.

Hear (or celebrate if you are a priest) many Masses as devoutly as possible. ONLY the Mass allows you to ADORE GOD as you MUST. ONLY the Mass obtains true REPARATION for your sins, original and actual. ONLY the Mass is a TRUE AND SUFFICIENT THANKSGIVING TO GOD. ONLY the Mass expresses true charity to others. IT alone obtains for them--especially those in Purgatory--God's graces and mercy.

"The Holy Mass is
the primary and indispensable Source
of the true Christian spirit,
and the faithful
will be filled with this spirit
only in proportion as they 'participate' in

[i.e. devoutly understand;
prayerfully attend;
and properly 'apply.']

the Sacred Mysteries."

Pope Saint Pius X

CHAPTER TWO

WHAT IS THE REAL MASS?

ONLY a sinner can pray the "Hail Mary." So also, ONLY a SINNER who sincerely acknowledges himself to be a sinner can profitably and prayerfully attend Mass, or celebrate Mass in the case of THE PRIEST.

In this meditation, strive to attain and to retain the salutary conviction of your own sinfulness, which is absolutely necessary for you in order to understand, appreciate and profit from attending Holy Mass--Christ's Unbloody Sacrifice for the Remission of your SINS.

The sacrifice of Calvary, the sacrifice of the Mass is called by David sacrificium justitiae, "the sacrifice of justice" (Ps. 1v. 5). It contains the Just One Himself. It contains justice and holiness. Only "IT" sanctifies souls.

The most holy sacrifice of the Mass is identical with that which was offered on the cross of Calvary: with this sole difference, that the sacrifice on the cross was bloody, and made once for all, and did on that one occasion satisfy fully for all the sins of the world; while the sacrifice of the altar is an unbloody sacrifice, which can be repeated a number of times, and was instituted in order to apply the ransom which Jesus paid for us on Calvary.

In each valid Mass, there is made not a mere representation, nor a simple commemoration of the passion and death of the Redeemer, but there happens, in a certain true sense, the selfsame most holy sacrifice which occurred on Calvary. It is Jesus Himself. It is His same Body. It is His same Blood. It is the same Jesus Who offered Himself at Calvary who now offers Himself at Mass.

The mystery of holy Mass, is no simple representation of a bygone event. Jesus Who then offered Himself upon Calvary, now offers Himself in the holy Mass. When you enter church to hear a valid Mass, you are going up as it were to Calvary, to be present at the death of the Redeemer. The Mystery of Holy Mass is not a simple representation or remembrance of an historical event, but it is the SAME SACRIFICE made in an unbloody manner as the Sacrifice on the Cross at Calvary where there occurred the actual shedding of Blood. The holy sacrifice of Mass is not a mere copy but is one with the sacrifice of the cross at Calvary.

THE TRUE PRIEST Who offers Mass is the God-Man, Our Lord Christ Jesus. The Victim is the Life of God--Jesus Christ-- offered to God. Recognize that the true celebrant is not the human priest but the adorable person of Our Lord Jesus Christ. As the primary offerer, not only did He institute this holy sacrifice, but He has also bestowed efficacy through His merits, because in each Mass He Himself deigns for our good to transubstantiate the bread and wine into His most holy Body and into His most precious Blood.

When you see THE PRIEST celebrating Mass at the altar, know that his highest dignity consists in being the minister of that invisible and eternal Priest, Our Redeemer Himself. Although THE PRIEST who celebrates may be wicked, seeing that the principal offerer is Christ Our Lord, and THE PRIEST as His minister is merely the representative of Christ, we have the good result that the sacrifice itself never ceases to be agreeable to God. Therefore, seeing that the principal offerer is Christ Our Lord, despite the humanity of THE PRIEST, (who may be with grave personal sin) the sacrifice is efficacious because THE PRIEST is nevertheless a substitute for Christ, Who is the Real Offerer.

This most perfect holy Priest offers to the Father His Body, His Blood, His Soul, and His Divinity--His whole self for us: and all this He does as many times as there are Masses celebrated in the whole world.

BE MORE THAN HEARERS!

Those who hear Mass not only perform the office of attendants, but likewise of offerers. They and THE PRIEST as a fellow man share a common priesthood as THEY "offer Christ to the Heavenly Father in as much as Christ dwells in them to offer Himself in sacrifice" (cf. Col 1:24).

YOU offer Christ only since and in as much as Christ lives in you (you live, not you but Christ in you). ONLY as such can and do you--yet, not you--offer Christ through THE PRIEST, who alone offers in persona Christi, the Holy Sacrifice of the Mass.

WHY do you attend Mass? Why are you involved in THE sacrifice?

For one thing, to avoid the JUST wrath of God. Indeed, the God of wrath still lives; BUT, as it were, because of Calvary He is clement to you. He forgives the sins of which you sincerely repent, BY HIS GRACES. The Mass scatters the clouds and renders heaven again serene! Behold the Heavenly Rainbow, pacifying the storms of divine justice!

Were it not for the holy Mass, at this moment the world would be in the abyss, unable to bear up under the mighty load of its iniquities. Mass is the potent prop that holds the world upon its base.

The just could exist more easily without the Sun than without THE Mass. Does not God spare each justified sinner for the sake of THE ONE JUST ONE AND HIS CONTINUING SACRIFICE OF THE MASS?

Does not God spare those of us of proper disposition from the Hell we so richly deserve because of THE SACRIFICE OF THE MASS? The Canonized Liturgy indeed is offered for our good--not, an earthbound good as described by NOEL's free-floating and banal offertory prayers--BUT that which is REALLY for our good.

Cardinal Silvio Oddi termed
the suppression of the
traditional Latin Mass as a

"crime for which history will never forgive the Church."

OUR CATHOLIC TRADITION
Vol. II, No. 2
May 1992

CHAPTER THREE

"FOR ALL"--THE GREATEST TREASON

When an American Priest says and truly or fully means "for all," in the words of consecration, THE CONSECRATION IS INVALID AND BLASPHEMOUS SACRILEGE RESULTS. The UNHOLY stands in the place of that which is supposed to be MOST HOLY.

Anti-Christ liberal--faith and worship destroying--legalists cringe and fight back with Satanic venom as they read these words. How can "our" wrong Church be wrong?

How can a church (in which--according to one of their own liberal heroes, Rev. Andrew Greeley, over 90% of alleged Catholics aren't Catholics since they disagree with at least one very basic Church Dogma) be wrong? How can such a church (as in "we are church") be wrong? The question should be: How could such a church of heretics--within which MOST of its bishops and priests have lost their office (in the eyes of God) and/or have been ipso facto excommunicated--be usually right or right on critical issues?

Now that I've painted the CORRECT background, let's go back to the original problem. The Novus Ordo English Liturgy (NOEL) has perverted its Novus Ordo Standard by "translating" PRO MULTIS as "for ALL."

Of course, legalistic apostates-within drag up reasons for this mega-evil distortion (much as American psychiatrists "justified" their decision to re-label sodomy as normal behavior.)

They said that "the original Mass or Masses" in Aramaic had to use "ALL" since Aramaic had no word for "many." However, in truth, Aramaic speaking people--as well as others--NEVER had to choose between, for example, giving away one or two cows or ALL cows since they didn't have any word(s) for "many." I often wonder why "they" aren't consistent to insist that Christ said ALL, not many, travel the broad road to eternal ruin.

Blind SIN-MOTIVATED reverence for reigning experts and their duped authorities has led some to choose and embrace the "FOR ALL" consecration "perversion." In doing so did not such people give allegiance to an apostate existential alleged Catholic Church in preference to the Real Catholic Church?

Regarding NOEL'S consecration, more than the Mass is involved. "For all" expresses the spirit of Anti-Christ and New Age Catholicism.

CATHOLIC FAITH is being grossly denied. Christ's Mass (as defined by Him and Him among us, the TRUE Church) is the EFFECTIVE SAVING ACTION. ALL are NOT saved. Therefore, a priest may NEVER say and mean "for ALL" at the consecration and remain a Catholic.

No one who believes in Basic Salvation Dogmas could go along with and not vehemently oppose the use of "for ALL" (even as a narrative statement.) ONLY a New Age Apostate would deny the Catholic Faith and espouse the heresy that ALL are saved. Only he would defend, promote or impose "for ALL" on Catholics--especially IN the Mass.

Obviously--in the light of Binding Catholic Faith--the Mass-Consecration must be expressed as being "for a multitude" or "for many" and NEVER "for ALL." In other words, "for ALL" must be dropped so that it can be acceptable to Catholics.

Also, the "conscious and fully meant" use of "for all" constitutes an anti-Christ betrayal. Such usage of these words confects (in the case of a priest who celebrates the Mass) SACRILEGE. Why? At such "Masses," would not such a celebrant be PRAYING THE HERESY OF UNIVERSAL SALVATION?

28

I will now consider a few of the apostates-within's "for ALL" arguments. First of all, in refutation of their "language-deficiency" argument, it is utterly ridiculous to allege that any language doesn't have a word or words to express "MANY." Language experts have shown that--as is the case with so many of "their" appeals to the remote past--"THEY" ARE TWISTING THE FACTS WE KNOW ABOUT THE ARAMAIC LANGUAGE IN ORDER TO VALIDATE THEIR LIES AS BEING THE TRUTH.

Regardless of their propaganda, it remains true that within today's NOEL, for a priest to say and fully mean "for all" constitutes a blasphemous and scandalous SACRILEGE. Why? He isn't speaking a primitive language. He's speaking contemporary English.

Now, to another strawman. On the authority of NOEL'S "mis-translation," modern experts "beg the question" as they present a "NOEL-IMITATING" Marionite Rite to validate their use of "for all." Regardless of where this rite's consecration words originate, IF they really mean "for ALL" then obviously this constitutes a "wrong-rite" and a BLASPHEMOUS and SCANDALOUS SACRILEGE.

Yes, Virginia, there are evil men in the Church and a "wrong-rite" can come into existence. Believe it or not, Virginia, NOEL's usage of "for all" constitutes a WRONG RITE. This wrong rite even exists with "official" approval.

Also, legalistic apostates-within or anti-Christs even drag out one of their worst enemies, St. Thomas, to prove that NOEL's said and meant "FOR ALL" Masses MUST BE VALID. Why? St. Thomas once stated that the valid form (essential words) of the Mass need only be: "This is My Body" and "This is My Blood."

Once these required words are uttered, they contend that

St. Thomas taught that Christ is made present automatically. According to their theory, THE PRIEST is reduced to some type of mechanical ROBOT. His intentions and the words surrounding what they define to be "per se validating" become insignificant IN THEIR VIEW. Do they not misuse St. Thomas?

Why do St. Thomas's exact words NOT apply to our situation? What would St. Thomas contend about NOEL's use of "for ALL?"

First of all, St. Thomas NEVER--even in his worst nightmares--envisaged a church being as ROTTEN as today's church. Today's church allows and "officially approves" GROSS ABERRATIONS WITHIN THE CONSECRATION MASS-PRAYERS. How much more rotten can any existential church be than to PERVERT "INTO HERESY OR SACRILEGE" the very words of consecration?

Of course, we are considering the most outstanding of the "consecration scandals." Cardinals Ottaviani and Bacci in their CRITICAL STUDY, and others as well, have pointed out other imposed aberrations. The "for all" aberration is the easiest one to perceive.

Certainly IF St. Thomas had the chance to address NOEL's GROSS DISTORTION OF THE MASS, he would go back to his definition of the Form of Consecration and apply that to NOEL's Mass Prayers--which, I repeat, in his worst nightmares he didn't think would ever come to be imposed upon the MOST HOLY MASS.

The FORM is that which signifies what is accomplished. "ALL of the words [of consecration, in our case] belong to the substance of the form..." (Summa Theologica, Pt. III, A 78, A. 3). "Therefore...any addition or suppression of words which DO NOT add to nor take away from the ESSENTIAL SENSE does not destroy the essence of the Sacrament" [or of the Mass] (III, Q 60).

"Positively stated," any addition or suppression of words which add to or take away from the ESSENTIAL SENSE or ESSENTIAL MEANING of the Mass AT LEAST DESTROY the essence of the Mass. No Mass happens.

Note well that St. Thomas addressed only additions or deletions. He didn't mention an "evil-substitution" of any words within the TOTAL FORM of consecration. Why? He didn't even have nightmares that such an utterly rotten church could ever materialize. He couldn't even imagine the "possibility" of such a HORROR.

When "for all" is said and fully meant--then not only is the Mass destroyed, it is also DEMONICALLY PERVERTED. Then, the UNHOLY "stands in the place of" or "is packaged as" THE MOST SACRED both didactically and sacramentally.

Such is my contention; and I'm very certain that this would also be St. Thomas's contention (after he recovered from the shock of perceiving "perverted Mass prayers" being "officially"--BUT NOT CANONICALLY--imposed upon Catholics).

We must note here that as Msgr. Gamber's book--which was fully endorsed and approved by Cardinal Ratzinger and two other "curial" cardinals--points out, the Novus Ordo (and, a fortiori, NOEL) DOES NOT AND CANNOT replace CL. In fact, according to Msgr. Gamber and implicitly the three Curial cardinals, the Novus Ordo--and, a fortiori, NOEL is not and cannot be an officially BINDING CATHOLIC RITUAL. Why? For one thing, as Msgr. Gamber points out, CATHOLIC RITUALS, as well as sacraments CAN'T be created by anyone--as has been clearly proven by the studies and "pollings" of NOEL's VICTIMS who are the "fruits" of NOEL.

"A day will come when the civilized world
will deny its God,
WHEN THE CHURCH WILL DOUBT
as Peter doubted.
She will be tempted to believe
that MAN HAS BECOME GOD...
IN OUR CHURCHES CHRISTIANS WILL
SEARCH IN VAIN
FOR THE RED LAMP WHERE GOD AWAITS THEM,
like Magdalen weeping before the EMPTY TOMB,
they will ask
'Where have THEY taken Him?' "

Pope Pius XII.

Msgr. Roche
"Pie XII devant l'histoire"
pp. 52-53, caps added.

> "About the 'RIGHTS OF MAN'
> as they are called,
> the people have heard enough:
>
>
> IT IS TIME WE SHOULD HEAR ABOUT THE RIGHTS OF GOD!"
>
>
> Pope Leo XIII
> Encyclical Letter TAMETSI

"The devil is always discovering something
novel against the truth"
Pope Leo the Great

"Let nothing new be introduced,
but only that which has been handed down."
Pope Benedict XV

CHAPTER FOUR

TO WHOM SHOULD I BE LOYAL?

At times I used to be tempted to question my tactics or my way of presenting the truth. Why should I give "the horrible truth" to those who are so unready for it that they not only reject the message but would like to stone the messenger?

Am I not leading others into their damnation? Why not be "nice and positive?" Why not please people?

As in all such states of spiritual turmoil, the best thing to do is to pray and be patient. Answers will come. God will provide. Finally, God answered and provided.

First of all, to whom am I "prophesying or speaking?" To a generation of present-day Americans. I am addressing the MOST ROTTEN OF SINNERS. Why should I as God's prophet be "nice and positive" to such as these?

Also, I should realize that MOST of them can NO more judge the truth or even what's good for them than a totally demented five year old. They are the apostates within. Well over eighty percent of American "Catholics" are in rank heresy. They aren't Catholics. Most of the other twenty or so percent are motivated by, controlled by or naturally respond as though they are influenced by--THE EVIL ATMOSPHERE WHICH ENVELOPES US.

People such as these cannot be my judges. As dedicated and blinded sinners, THEIR opinions and sentiments are "non-Godly" or Satanic.

As I look into past history, I see that those who were called by God to be prophets spoke--NOT FOR MEN--but TO humans FOR God. That's a prophet's job (and ALL of us are called to be prophets).

Nearly ALWAYS true prophets were rejected. Those who rejected the classical biblical prophets were much more religious than those who live in our times. Today's American "Catholics" are so awesomely wicked that having received the light and the grace, THEY live in rejection of both of these.

Actually, my only problem should be WHY AM I ALLOWED TO EXIST IN SUCH AN AWESOMELY WICKED CATHOLIC CHURCH? I should fear that I have failed God.

In answer to my fears and for my consolation, God shows me that I am improving and "they" are worsening. Why? As time goes on, I am being opposed more often and more strongly. I thank God for this great gift.

YET, why should I oppose people? Why not "love" them? Why not speak softly? Why not be prudent (as "they" define prudence) and positive?

One answer is found in the ACTUAL speeches of Jesus and the proven prophets (those who speak God's Relevant Message so effectively as to elicit an OUCH or an AMEN). Jesus Himself failed to please MEN. At one point, nearly all of Jesus' disciples left because He required the people to believe that He could be eaten.

During the final hours of His life, nearly all forsook Him AS HE DIED WITNESSING TO THE AWESOME TRUTH--each man (except for the Blessed Virgin Mary) is a rotten sinner whose only hope is accepting and conforming to the Suffering Saving Event and Person.

Indeed, Jesus the Light entered the WORLD and it rejected Him. Indeed, the Light came unto His chosen People (the Jews) and they rejected Him. Naturally, MEN HATE THE TRUTH.

However, to fulfill God's Will, Jesus came and showed forth the light. It is my HONOR and not my HORROR to imitate Jesus and to be as Jesus--to be HIS light to others.

In my "better moments" I realize that in as much as I am like Christ, I too will be rejected; I too will be persecuted; and eventually, I hope that I too will be put to death for His sake. My only real shame is that in this most rotten of generations I HAVE NOT YET SUFFERED CHRIST'S "FATE."

A SPECIAL LESSON

I have always been impressed by Jeremiah, the Prophet. He was weak, like me. He too was a "cry baby."

In fact, he was one of the "cryingest" cry babies that ever lived. Jeremiah regretted that he was ever born. All cursed him--so "felt" this great true prophet of God (Jer 15:10).

Then God gave him a retreat. He devoured God's Word. Today we have so much more of the Bible than Jeremiah had. How much more of a retreat we.can make. Jeremiah became transformed from within (he ate God's words, v. 16). A new Jeremiah emerged. A blessed Jeremiah emerged.

The new Jeremiah NO LONGER WAS AFFECTED BY THE PEOPLE'S DEMANDS, CONTEMPT, HATRED, RIDICULE, REJECTION AND PERSECUTION (Jer 15;19;20). He had become a brass wall to the people. THIS was his blessing!

No longer would he bother to please the people. No longer would he be affected by their words--words such as the following: "You didn't make us feel good... You're NEGATIVE... My God is loving... Most disagree with you... Why can't you be loving and nice?... Why don't you speak nicely to us?..."

You too are called to be--nay, demanded to be--A PROPHET. You will only survive and prosper as such IF you receive "the Jeremiah blessing" from God--IF AND WHEN He makes you into "a brass wall to the people (v. 20)."

A LOYAL PAPIST?

In reading this book, you will be challenged as to IF and HOW you believe in Christ's One and Only Church (in which you should believe since you believe in Christ). The focal point of many of your psycho-spiritual KRISES (basic moral TESTS) will be THE POPE.

As Catholics we believe that ONLY the Pope occupies the Apostolic See, the Holy See of St. Peter. As such, he takes the place of St. Peter. St. Peter lives among us when the Pope speaks or acts as Pope.

In general Catholics follow the Apostolic See or the Chair of St. Peter. Symbolically the SEDES (special papal chair) is no longer used. It is covered with dust and hidden in some dark corner of the Vatican.

Since 1958, no pope has spoken with full (or even adequate) papal authority (not just "ex cathedra" BUT as pope AUTHORITATIVELY) to papally bind. Why 1958? From Pope John XXIII on, THE POPES THEMSELVES explicitly, and in effect, have issued their own DISCLAIMERS to speaking AUTHORITATIVELY AS POPES (i.e. to bind on earth in virtue of their being popes).

Why 1958? "The Third Secret is to be made known to the world by 1960 AT THE LATEST... It will be clear at that time why that date is chosen." --God's Fatima Message.

Since then "it" has become clearer. We have, as St. Peter observed, "The more sure word of prophecy" (II Pe 1:19).

We are hungry children. We desperately need THE HOLY FATHER to feed us. However, the modern popes haven't given us adequate food.

We desperately need a pope like Pope St. Pius V who fed God's children and "kicked out" God's enemies from Christ's Church. Nothing less than this is adequate!

As it were, the truly faithful are NOW on emergency rations--regarding the PRESENT. We do not follow popes as MEN--we follow popes as popes. We want a pope who will "pope."

Even when a pope speaks on faith and morals--WE DO NOT HAVE TO FOLLOW HIM. Only when he speaks authoritatively as pope do we owe him obedience UNLESS, of course, he is reiterating what all Catholics MUST believe (sensus fidelium or previous papally-binding decrees).

Therefore, we can conclude that ANY NEW AND NOVEL papal teaching does not bind us UNLESS it is issued with true papal authority.

For example, Pope Pius XII in 1957 (as recorded in THE ACTA APOSTOLICAE SEDIS) said that when a person can't answer yes or no, he shouldn't be given Extreme Unction since the sacraments were meant for living human beings. This papal statement has been used by modern "Catholic bio-ethicians" to promote the sinful notions of "brain-dead" and "brain-birth."

THEREFORE, YOU MUST BE AS WISE AS A SERPENT. ESPECIALLY, YOU MUST JUDGE EVERY "POST-1960" APPARENTLY OR ACTUALLY NEW AND NOVEL PAPAL STATEMENT--AS REGARDS ITS FIDUCIAL "PAPAL BINDINGNESS"--IN THE LIGHT OF PAST FIDUCIALLY BINDING PAPAL STATEMENTS.

THEN REJECT OR ACCEPT SUCH NON-INFALLIBLE STATEMENTS. YOUR PROPERLY CATHOLIC-FORMED CONSCIENCE MUST BE YOUR GUIDE. YOU MUST FOLLOW SUCH A CONSCIENCE REGARDING WHICH BASICS YOU BELIEVE OR REFUSE TO BELIEVE.

Also, the bold assertion that QUO PRIMUM as issued by Pope St. Pius V is NULL AND VOID--seems to be RASH AND DANGEROUS. If one can REJECT the clearly official and binding statements of THIS encyclical--WHAT ENCYCLICALS MUST ONE FOLLOW OR WHAT ENCYCLICAL COULDN'T BE REJECTED?

Indeed, the pope is pope; HOWEVER, must not each pope follow the binding papal decrees of his predecessors? IF any pope could deny and disobey any binding papally-decreed teaching, then would not the Church NO LONGER be ONE-- semper, ubique et pro omnibus? Indeed, the Church's canonized practice of DEMANDING conformity to the "safest sacramental opinion" WAS and remains a VERY WISE PRACTICE.

WE desperately need a Catholic theology for our times on this problem. St. Vincent of Lerins assured us that in times of almost complete "fiducial rot," we must go back to the past. We need thousands of such Saint Vincents.

St. Peter was reprimanded by St. Paul for DOING EVIL (by refusing to eat with gentile Catholics). WE need millions of Saint Pauls!

Modern popes (since 1958 or so) aren't incapable of SIN. IN FACT, too much of what they say, do or permit AS POPES is not only sinful and NOT to be believed (or followed IF it makes one sin); BUT, is also GROSSLY SCANDALOUS.

These are times when one could contend that IGNORANCE IS BLISS. Those who live simple lives in blissful ignorance of what MODERN POPES have said or have neglected to do or say APPARENTLY ARE BLESSED.

Nearly all of us were--at one time--blissfully ignorant. However, every time we see a challenging relevant truth about the Church and IMPLICITLY about the present pope; OR about the pope's actions or failures to act, we have a "modern fiducial crisis."

Each such crisis TESTS YOU. Will you follow the Pope as Pope or will you follow this Pope as Man? Your choices are inevitable. Your choices can damn you to eternal Hell or strengthen your faith.

May God bless you with overwhelming graces in such crises, which are peculiar to the times after 1960. May God lead you to be prudent and patient with those who are in blissful ignorance.

Realize that what you don't know can DAMN YOU TO HELL WHEN IT IS WHAT GOD DEMANDS YOU TO HAVE KNOWN. "Certain ignorances" MUST BE resolved or removed under pain of mortal sin.

May God bless you in these the worst times of Catholicism. May God help you to know and to persevere in THE CATHOLIC FAITH.

"...Specifically, do we warn all persons in authority of whatever dignity or rank, and command them as a matter of strict obedience never to use or permit any ceremonies of Mass prayers other than the ones contained in this Missal...

At no time in the future can a priest, whether secular or order priest, ever be forced to use any other way of saying Mass. And in order once and for all to preclude any scruples of conscience and fear of ecclesiastical penalties and censures, we declare herewith that it is by virtue of our Apostolic authority that we decree and prescribe that this present order and decree of ours is to last in PERPETUITY, and never at a future date can it be revoked or amended legally...

And if, nevertheless, anyone would dare attempt any action contrary to this order of ours, handed down for all times, let him know that he has incurred the wrath of Almighty God, and of the Blessed Apostles Peter and Paul."

Pope St. Pius V
QUO PRIMUM

CHAPTER FIVE

THE CANONIZED LITURGY:
MEN TO GOD THROUGH CHRIST-PRIEST

NOVUS ORDO ENGLISH LITURGY:
CHRIST-HUMANS RECALL, CELEBRATE AND COMMUNE

The Canonized Liturgy (CL) and the Novus Ordo English Liturgy (NOEL) come from, and express opposing "theologies." In fact, CL centers on God. NOEL focuses on MAN, MAN AS GOD or MAN AS CHRIST (the anointed of God).

CL originates from, sustains and terminates in THEO-logy. NOEL originates from, sustains and terminates in an HOMO-logy (man-centered-ness).

Only ignorance or a prevailing demonic delusion prevent one from seeing the obvious. Does not NOEL lead one to the CULT OF MAN? Is not worship--as the acknowledgement of WORTH--shifted from God as its object to MAN?

TO GOD THROUGH CHRIST-PRIEST

CL, as all official and approved CHRIST-BASED MASS-LITURGIES (originating from TRULY apostolic tradition and not a fabricated LIVING apostolic tradition) PRAY through Christ-priest to God; and, receive from God SALVATION, through Christ-priest. MAN, by and in himself, is and remains powerless unto fulfillment. MAN, the adored object of NOEL, is powerless, graceless, a Hell-destined SINNER--and that's the truth.

MAN'S--actually each individual's--only HOPE is Christ-priest. ONLY Christ saves. Christ saves ONLY AS HE DESIRES and whom HE desires.

CL'S EUCHARIST--thanksgiving--is THE SAVING DEED AND PERSON, CHRIST. This EUCHARIST can only come about by a validly ordained priest with the proper intention and using the proper (Christ-defined and classical-church-ratified) matter and form.

Each SUCH priest IS and ACTS IN PERSONA CHRISTI. Each such priest is Christ-priest.

Therefore, it is fitting, proper and necessary (whenever possible) that each CL Mass be in front of a tabernacle. On earth, ONLY in the tabernacle does DIVINITY DWELL SACRAMENTALLY--that DIVINITY TO WHOM THE CHRIST-PRIEST OFFERS AND RECEIVES THE EUCHARISTIC SACRIFICE AND PRESENCE.

Indeed, THE Mass-prayer is to God. Why symbolize, express and PRAY the opposite? Why introduce an alien and opposing theology? Why introduce, symbolize and pray a so alien theology that it becomes an HOMO-logy?

NOEL "PRAYS" MAN TO MAN AS CHRIST-HUMANS

NOEL is devoted to MAN individual/community. NOEL is NOT devoted to God or to Christ-priest.

Look at NOEL'S "symbolism"-- its positioning of chief presider and those presided for; its "total uncomfortableness" with DIVINITY (with God in the tabernacle); its turning its back on GOD (in the tabernacle); its kicking GOD out of HIS temple; its devotedness to humans which reaches the zenith of idolatry as each is called "Christ" at the expense of the Holy Eucharist; etc. ad nauseam.

THIS and so much more expresses the homology of NOEL. Praise to MAN! Praise to liturgy--the work of MAN. Move over God. Move out of HUMAN'S way.

Man's ugly fist is thrown into God's face. WHEN will God's vengeance strike? (cf. Apoc 8)

Is this not the Liturgical Beast (of Apoc 13)? Is this not MAN (6) praised as God (666)? Thrice-praised HUMAN (666) takes God's place. The abominable desolation is HERE. NOEL is HERE!

Can we not read into the startling words of Pope Paul VI an inference that GOD no longer is being worshipped in HIS Temple? "The (incense) smoke of Satan has entered the sanctuary of the Catholic Church" --Pope Paul VI.

IS NOEL CATHOLIC?

Today, NOEL redefines "liturgy." For NOELITES, "liturgy" is now THE WORK OF MAN. How vain!

How utterly useless! How infinitely and eternally detrimental is it for MAN to "sacrilege" LITURGY, which is the God-commanded and God-bestowed DEED of praising God.

Let's go back to basics since basics are being denied and vilified. Why did GOD make YOU?

The canonized, dogmatic and authentic catechisms of the Catholic Church tell us that EACH OF US IS CREATED TO KNOW, LOVE AND MINISTER TO OR TO SERVE GOD. Period! YOU (who read this book) will do this--eternally in Heaven or eternally in Hell.

God is central. God is "IT." Only God is worthwhile. ONLY God is to be served or worshipped. The Novus Ordo's greatest sacrilegious SIN is to deny this--in spirit and in truth; as well as, in purpose and in execution.

The Anti-Christ leads us to know, love and liturgize or worship MAN. God is dethroned. MAN is enthroned (cf. Rv 13).

GOD made YOU to know, love and serve HIM. IF you can't fulfill your purpose to be an eternal God-adorer: THEN, you'll be infinitely agonized burning refuse. There's no other possibility for YOU.

Either way--in eternal Heaven or in eternal Hell--YOU will glorify God. New Age Catholicism (NAC) preaches that you are as God and will always show forth God's goodness. For NAC, all is POSITIVE!

The existence and popularity of NAC's mega-lie indicate the extent and depth of MAN'S sinful state. The darkness rejects the light unto damnation.

Grieve with the Sacred Hearts of Jesus and Mary. Grieve over the utmost sinfulness of MAN--even of the modern popes who in their papal statements apparently have preached and endorsed the inevitable glory of MAN. How such gross papal betrayal grieves the Sacred Hearts.

You, man, are a SINNER. For all eternity, AT BEST, you'll be a saved sinner; and, AT WORST a God-damned sinner. That's the truth. That's Catholic Dogma. Believe it or be damned.

Only one human person is SINLESS. Only one has a nature and person which are sinless. Only one is the Blessed Virgin Mary.

You and I are sinners--by birth, by inclination, by deed; and, even in habits, both known and unknown. Will YOU renounce New Age Catholicism (NAC), the EVIL SPIRIT within NOVUS ORDO ENGLISH LITURGY (NOEL) and the spirit of this world? Will YOU admit YOU are a SINNER? Only then, will YOU have a chance to be saved from the infinite agony of eternal Hell.

Naturally, or by our own efforts we are Hell-bound sinners. God's Bible tells us so.

After THE fall, after Adam's federal sin, after original sin, each human is born without a right to Heaven. Each needs to accept and to live salvation from Christ Jesus as HE defined it to be--through Him and His one and only Church.

ALL of the non-Jewish liturgies--expressions of man's meta-physical desires and hopes--were (and still are) sinful and useless. Why?

They were and still are, LITURGY--the works of men. As such, they are vain--arising from and expressing sinful pride and totally ineffective.

The God-given Jewish liturgy (the God-commanded act of praising God) foreshadowed Reality. At best, in itself, it WAS (before Christ) poor and deficient (Gal 4:9).

After Christ, this liturgy deteriorates into being merely a MAN-liturgy. It joins the vain works of fellow idolaters, those who worship false gods or who worship God falsely.

Enough of MAN and MAN-LITURGY. Enough of MAN and all of HIS vain works and pomps.

Enough of THE NEGATIVE. Let's now look at THE one and only liturgy or sacrifice by which we can become saved sinners--saved from the eternal Hell we so naturally deserve.

> "WHEN A FOULNESS INVADES THE WHOLE CHURCH...
> WE MUST RETURN TO THE CHURCH OF THE PAST."
>
> St. Vincent of Lerins
> THE HIDDEN TREASURE
> TAN PUBLISHERS, INC.

"Such is the value of Tradition that
even Encyclicals and other documents of
the ordinary teaching of the Sovereign Pontiff
are only infallible in those teachings
that are confirmed by Tradition, or by a continuous
teaching under various Popes
and over a long period.

If therefore an act of the ordinary magisterium of a Pope
disagrees with the teaching guaranteed
by the magisterial tradition of several Popes
and for a considerable time,
it should not be accepted...

Therefore, in full harmony with the Church,
all priests may continue
to celebrate the traditional Mass of St. Pius V."

Bishop Antonio de Castro Mayer
Brazil
Pastoral Letters: 1971-72

CHAPTER SIX

THE HOLY MASS HAS:

TWO DIVISIONS; SIX PARTS;

THIRTY-THREE PRAYER SEGMENTS

There are two major divisions to THE PRIEST'S Mass--the Unbloody Sacrifice of Calvary OR Calvary "re-done" out of its "proper" space and time and brought into THE PRIEST'S space and time as best that God can do this for us who dwell this side of our death. In the first division of the Mass, THE PRIEST--who ALONE celebrates Mass--prays to God and receives God's words, which he shares with the congregation and then "applies" to them in his sermon.

The first division of the Mass is open to the properly curious or those preparing to enter THE one and only church of God. The second division centers on THE Eucharist Itself--Sacrifice and Sacrament. This "second division" is open only to those who--as best we can ascertain--are Christ's own, at least BY PERSONAL RESOLUTION OR INTENT AND BY GOD'S ELECTION OR PROVIDENCE.

There are six parts of the Mass--two in the first division and four in the second. Why? The Mass is on behalf of or FOR men whose number is six (since man was created on the sixth day). The Mass is the one and only Saving-ACT out of which "remains" the Saving-PERSON.

The Mass is Heaven's Life or Focus (Apoc 5:12). The Mass is THE one and only life or source of life for God's ELECT. Most aptly does St. Paul assure us of the FACT that gross sinners (those in mortal sin) receive THE Source, Sustainer and Fruit of the Mass (Jesus Christ) UNTO THEIR DAMNATION OR GREATER DAMNATION (1 Col 11:29).

Reflecting the years of Christ's Redemptive Life, we have thirty-three prayer-segments in the Canonized or Classical Mass of the Latin Rite of the Roman Catholic Church. Let's illustrate our observations.

FIRST DIVISION:

MASS OF THE CATECHUMENS

FIRST PART: PRAYERS TO GOD

1) Asperges or Vidi Aquam or Procession to the Altar

2) Prayers at the Foot of the Altar

3) On Ascending to the Altar, Priest recites Aufer a nobis--

4) Priest kisses the Altar stone and recites the Oramus te--

5) The Introit: Proper No. 1 (A "proper" is a reading or prayer that is designated for or "peculiar to" the particular Mass that THE PRIEST chooses to celebrate).

6) The Kyrie

7) The Gloria

SECOND PART: INSTRUCTIONS FROM GOD

8) The Collect: Proper No. 2

9) The Epistle: Proper No. 3

10) The Gradual, Alleluia, Tract, and Sequence: Proper No. 4

11) Munda cor meum--

12) The Gospel: Proper No. 5

13) The Credo

SECOND DIVISION:

MASS OF THE FAITHFUL

THIRD PART

THE "PRIEST-CHRIST" OFFERS CHRIST TO GOD
(From the Offering of Christ to the Preface)

14) Dominus vobiscum--Oremus, then the Offertory antiphon: Proper No. 6

15) Offering of Christ

    a)   Receive, O Holy Father (Suscipe sancte Pater)--
    b)   O God Who in a wonderful manner
           (Deus, qui humanae)--
    c)   We offer unto Thee, O Lord, (Offerimus tibi)--
    d)   In the spirit of humility (In spiritu)--
    e)   Come, O Sanctifier, (Veni, sanctificator)--
    f)   High Mass only: Incensing of the Bread and Wine
         and the Faithful

                    Four Prayers: Through the intercession--
                                   May this incense--
                                   Let my prayer--
                                   May the Lord--

16) <u>Washing of the Hands:</u> Lavabo inter innocentes--

17) <u>Prayer to the Most Holy Trinity:</u> Suscipe, sancta Trinitas--

18) <u>Brethren, pray:</u> Orate fratres--<u>Secret:</u> <u>Proper No. 7</u> and concluding Amen

FOURTH PART:

THE HEART OF THE PRIEST'S MASS
(From the Preface to the Lord's Prayer)

19) <u>Preface to the Canon</u> (A "canon" is the official and binding "way" to pray the Mass as THE SAVING ACT).

    a)   Dominus Vobiscum--
    b)   Preface (variable)
    c)   Sanctus--

20) <u>The Immediate Preparation Prayers</u>

    a)   Prayer to God to Accept the Offerings (Te Igitur)--
    b)   The Diptychs: <u>The Church Militant</u> (Pope, Bishop, all Catholics and specific faithful); the "diptychs" are prayers which show for whom Christ is offered. The Church Triumphant (Blessed Mother, St. Joseph [1962 Missal Romanum] Apostles, Martyrs, Popes and Saints)
    c)   Prayers in preparation for the Consecration (Hanc Igitur)-
    d)   Prayer that bread and wine become the Body and Blood of Christ (Quam oblationem)--

21) <u>THE ACTUAL SAVING-ACT</u>--or the Unbloody Sacrifice and Major Elevation

a) Consecration of the bread: Who the day before He suffered (Qui pridie quam pateretur)--

b) Consecration of the wine: In like manner, after He had supped (Simili modo postquam)

22) <u>Oblation of the Victim to God</u>

a) Wherefore, O Lord (Unde et memores)--
b) Upon which vouchsafe (Supra quae)--
c) We most humbly beseech (Supplices te)--

23) <u>The Diptychs AS Offering Christ FOR: Church Suffering, Militant and Triumphant</u>

a) Be mindful also, O Lord (Memento etiam)--
b) And to us sinners (Nobis quoque)--
c) Through whom, O Lord (Per quem haec)--

24) <u>End of the Solemn and Official Canon and Minor Elevation</u>

a) Through Him and with Him (Per ipsum et cum ipso)--

FIFTH PART:

Communion
(From the Lord's Prayer to the Ablutions)

25) <u>The Lord's Prayer</u> and <u>Libera nos</u>

a) Let us pray (Oremus)--; Our Father (Pater Noster)--
b) Deliver us (Libera nos)--

26) <u>The Fraction of the Sacred Host</u> (Christ "under the appearance of" bread)

a) The peace of the Lord (Pax Domini)--

b)   May this mingling (Haec commixtio)--

27) <u>The Agnus Dei</u>
   a)   Lamb of God (Agnus Dei)--

28) <u>Prayers in preparation for Holy Communion</u>

   a)   O Lord Jesus Christ Who said to Thy Apostles
        (Domine Jesu Christe, qui dixisti Apostolis)--
   b)   O Lord Jesus Christ, Son of the living God (Domine
        Christe, Fili Dei vivi)--

29) <u>Communion of the Priest</u>

   a)   I will take of the Bread of Heaven (Panem caelestem
        accipiam)--
   b)   Lord, I am not worthy (Domine, non sum dignus)--
   c)   May the Body of our Lord (Corpus Domini nostri)--
        Priest receives Christ, the Sacred Host (Victim)
        "under the appearance of" bread
   d)   What shall I render to the Lord (Quid retribuam
        Domino)--
   e)   May the Blood of our Lord (Sanguis Domini nostri)--
        Priest receives Christ "under the appearance of" wine
   f)   Servers say <u>Confiteor Deo</u>--
   g)   <u>Priest gives absolution:</u> May Almighty God
        (Misereatur vestri)--
        May the Almighty and Merciful Lord (Indulgentiam
        absolutionem)--
        Priest holds up Host and says Ecce Agnus Dei
        (Behold the Lamb of God)
        Domine non sum dignus (Lord I am not worthy).
        In administering Holy Communion, THE PRIEST
        says "Corpus Domini nostri Jesu Christi custodiat
        animam tuam in vitam aeternam. Amen."
        (May the Body of Our Lord Jesus Christ
        preserve your soul to life everlasting. Amen.)

SIXTH PART:

THANKSGIVING
(From Communion to end of Mass)

30) <u>Prayers during Ablutions</u> (washing of Priest's fingers)

    a)   Grant O Lord (Quod ore Sumpsimus)
    b)   May Thy Body, O Lord (Corpus tuum Domine)--
    c)   Communion Antiphon: Proper No. 8
    d)   Dominus vobiscum--then Postcommunion: Proper No. 9

31) <u>The Ite Missa est, Placeat and Blessing</u>

    a)   Dominus vobiscum--
    b)   Ite Missa est (Go you are sent) or if there is no Gloria:
        Benedicamus Domino (Let us bless the Lord) or at
        Masses for the dead: Requiescant in pace (May they
        rest in peace)
    c)   May the homage (Placeat tibi)--
    d)   May the almighty God bless you (Benedicat vos
        omnipotens Deus)--

32) <u>The Last Gospel</u> (John 1. 1-14)

    a)   Dominus vobiscum (The Lord be with you)
        Initium sancti Evangelii secundum Joannem (The
        beginning of the holy Gospel according to St. John)
    b)   In the beginning was the Word (In principio
        erat Verbum)--

33) <u>Prayers after Low Mass</u>

    a)   Hail Mary, Hail Holy Queen,
        O God Our Refuge and Our Strength
        St. Michael the Archangel
        Most Sacred Heart of Jesus
    b)   Your own prayers of "Eucharistic Thanksgiving" after
        Holy Mass

Pope St. Pius V established the Canonized Liturgy
to be said FOR ALL TIME.

It alone is to be THE Liturgy of the Roman Rite.

Pope St. Pius V granted a PERPETUAL INDULT--

valid "FOR ALWAYS"

to celebrate the traditional Mass
freely, licitly, without scruple of conscience,
punishment, sentence or censure."

Papal Bull QUO PRIMUM

PART TWO

PRAY THE HOLY MASS

PRAYER BY PRAYER

"The just could exist more easily
without the Sun
than without THE MASS.

Does not God spare each justified sinner
for the sake of
THE ONE JUST ONE
AND
HIS CONTINUING SACRIFICE OF THE MASS?"

St. Leonard of Port Maurice
THE HIDDEN TREASURE
TAN PUBLISHERS

INTRODUCTION

ONLY THE PRIEST celebrates or says the Mass. No one else does. Period. Any other teaching is HERESY. Any contrary practice or liturgy is HERETICAL.

However, you ATTEND Mass. Such attendance isn't trivial. It's the greatest thing you can do here on earth.

It will be "THE THING" done eternally in Heaven. THE MASS--AS THE LAMB THAT WAS ONCE SLAIN-- CONSTITUTES THE "ADORED ESSENCE" OF HEAVEN for rational creatures. Read Apoc. 5:12.

As YOU attend Mass capitalize on this great opportunity to PRAY THE HOLY MASS BY KNOWING AND UNDERSTANDING THE PRIEST'S PRAYERS; AND, BY PRAYING THEM AS ONE WHO IS PRIVILEGED TO ATTEND MASS. Unless you are a priest, you do NOT celebrate Mass.

What is PRAYING? Praying is LIFTING UP YOUR MIND AND HEART TO GOD (not to MAN as is the thrust of NOEL). The "community" is a set of individuals with a common property. As such, community CANNOT pray. Only individuals PRAY or don't PRAY.

"PRAY THE HOLY MASS" as Pope St. Pius X urged YOU. Do as THE SAINT said. Obey THE Pope!

ONLY individuals can pray or not pray the Holy Mass. YOU either pray the Holy Mass or YOU DON'T pray the Holy Mass.

Lift up your mind and heart to God AS THE ESSENCE (or meaning) AND THE ACTUAL PRIEST-PRAYERS OF THE HOLY MASS LEAD YOU. PRAY THE HOLY MASS- -THE CANONIZED MASS OF THE LATIN CATHOLIC RITE.

Pray that same Holy Mass which made men and women like you into SAINTS throughout the Church's centuries-- "dogmatically climaxing" in Popes St. Pius V and St. Pius X; and, as it were, "Christ-Priest climaxing" in the only stigmatized priest, Padre Pio, who died two weeks before he was to be forced to say the Novus Ordo Liturgy.

Be mega-positive! Become a saint. Pray the Holy Mass-- that Mass which "produced" the Church's most outstanding SAINTS. Let "it" make you into an outstanding saint; or, at least, let THE Sacrifice keep YOU from going to eternal Hell.

The following chapter is written to help YOU to PRAY THE HOLY MASS as you attend Mass or as YOU prepare to attend Mass by making the PRIEST'S PRAYERS your prayers--by helping you to lift up your mind and heart to GOD. Do so by appropriately joining YOUR mind and heart to those prayer-sentiments which are expressed or implied by the actual PRIEST-PRAYERS of THE HOLY MASS.

"Let Christ's mind and heart be in YOU as it is expressed in Christ's Sacrifice (Phil 3:5-8)." PRAY CHRIST'S HOLY MASS. PRAY THE HOLY MASS.

"LEX ORANDI--LEX CREDENDI."

"WHAT" we pray or liturgically express

determines "what" we believe--

for our salvation

OR

for our damnation.

NOTE:

In this very important section, as you pray the Mass prayer by prayer--you'll notice that I occasionally leave out a prayer or so. I do so because my main purpose is to have you pray the Holy Mass by LIFTING UP YOUR MIND AND HEART TO GOD in a Mass-related way.

THE PRIEST must say each prayer. YOU need not do so. Your ADVANTAGE is that you can focus on properly lifting up your mind and heart to God and not be concerned about praying each and every Mass prayer.

You may wish to meditate on the Mass Prayers before or during Mass. If you do so during Mass, limit yourself to meditating on only a few of the Mass Prayers.

As time goes on, you'll be able to choose your favorite meditations. These should help you to pray the Mass as best you can.

CHAPTER SEVEN

PRAY THE HOLY MASS--PRAYER BY PRAYER

INTROIBO AD ALTARE DEI

"Introibo ad altare Dei..." I will enter unto the altar of God. THE PRIEST, as Christ, is here to bring SALVATION to Christ's elect and Christ's elect to SALVATION--not as modern mega-heretical "Catholics" understand the liturgy to be; but as the Mass really is.

HERE in this priest-centered NOW comes the Saving Action out of which and with which is the Saving Presence. This Saving Person is Jesus Christ, God and man. HERE is your ONLY REAL HOPE to be spared an eternity of Hell. HERE is Salvation.

In the beginning God made whatever began. WASTE, VOID, DESTITUTION; DEATH. God the Father breathed forth--"Holy Spirit-wise"--and spoke the Son: "'LET LIGHT BE.' LIGHT WAS and it was good (Genesis v. 1-2)."

In these two verses of Genesis is capsuled REALITY. You, I and each rational person is on earth to CHOOSE. The Salvation-rejecting choice has been made and tends to be ratified. Naturally, you and I are destined to be eternally part of the TOHU-BOHU, the darkest desolation. Broad is the way to HELL and many go that way.

Only by somehow being the freely God-chosen effect of, positively effected by, cooperating with and brought into GOD'S REPARATION--God's re-paring of creation--can any of us escape our natural "Hell-boundedness" or our Adam-chosen destiny. Holy Mary, pray for us, SINNERS.

HERE, at this valid Mass a valid priest is given the privilege of bringing THE ONLY SALVATION into HIS time and space. "Introibo ad altare Dei..." I, THE PRIEST, will go into and bring down THE LAMB THAT WAS SLAIN, HE WHO IS FOREVER THE ONE AND ONLY ADORED FOCUS OF HEAVEN, outside of which is Satan-evoked, Adam-chosen and "natural-man-destined" ETERNAL HELL.

Contemporary man-created community is a powerless abstraction--a creation of mega-heretical modernists. The community can huff and puff or rant and rave BUT it is entirely impotent to say Mass.

Only a properly ordained priest with proper matter and form and with the proper intention says Mass. Mass is ONLY THE PRIEST'S prayer, at which a congregation may be privileged to attend. Many of the Council of Trent's dogmatic condemnations were aimed at various Protestant expressions which weakened or denied the BINDING CATHOLIC BELIEF that the Mass is THE PRIEST'S prayer.

Modern proud mega-heretical "Catholics" can't accept this dogmatic truth. THEY reject Christ and His Plan. Thus, they are more firmly and more deeply damned to eternal Hell.

Are you humble enough to accept God's Plan? Or, do you wish to decide what is true or false and what is good or bad?

If you can accept God's Revelation, thank God. Appreciate it. Pray it. Tell others about it.

Lift up your mind and heart to Christ. As one who ATTENDS, join in THE PRIEST'S PRAYER. It is prayed for you.

"By means of the unbloody immolation
(in the august sacrifice of the altar)

the High Priest (Jesus Christ)
continues to do that
which He already did
on the Cross
by offering Himself
to the Eternal Father
as the only and
most acceptable Victim."

Pope Pius XII
<u>MEDIATOR DEI</u>
1947

Ordo Missæ

MASS OF THE CATECHUMENS

IN nómine Patris, ✝ et Fílii, et Spíritus Sancti. Amen.

P. Introíbo ad altáre Dei.
S. Ad Deum qui lætíficat juventútem meam.

THE PRIEST enters the sanctuary of the altar--"in the name of God." NOEL's facilitators are MAN-centered. "Good morning, WE gather to celebrate..."

Priests of the Canonized Liturgy are God-centered because they are God-oriented. THEY are at Mass in the name--in the power--of God, not MAN. They function in God's name, not MAN's.

Catholic prayers are begun with the Sign of the Cross. Here, the Sign of the Cross is a profession of faith in the great Sacrifice of the Mass which is being celebrated by THE PRIEST.

The Ordinary of the Mass

MASS OF THE CATECHUMENS

In the name of the Father, ✝ and of the Son, and of the Holy Ghost. Amen.

Priest: I will go in unto the Altar of God.
Server: To God, who giveth joy to my youth.

"I will go unto the altar of God." Standing at the foot of the altar THE PRIEST is reflecting on what he is about to do. In the words of Padre Pio, THE PRIEST is about to "butcher God" on behalf of sinners.

THE PRIEST is going to the ALTAR OF SACRIFICE and not to a mere table. By its nature, St. John Chrysostom said, "The altar is a unique stone, for it is sanctified by the fact of the presence of Jesus Christ."

That is why, at High Mass, THE PRIEST having kissed the altar, pays honour to it by censing it. In the Apocalypse incense is seen as a symbol of the prayers of the Saints. Essentially and primarily, incense as placed on the altar gives forth pleasing fragrance to God in Heaven. How apt a symbol of the Sacrifice of Christ to the Father on our behalf!

Judica Me — Psalm 42

JÚDICA me, Deus, et discérne causam meam de gente non sancta: ab hómine iníquo, et dolóso érue me.

S. Quia tu es, Deus, fortitúdo mea: / quare me repulísti, / et quare tristis incédo, / dum afflígit me inimícus?

P. Emítte lucem tuam, et veritátem tuam: ipsa me deduxérunt, et adduxérunt in montem sanctum túum, et in tabernácula tua.

S. Et introíbo ad altáre Dei: / ad Deum qui laetíficat juventútem meam.

P. Confitébor tibi in cíthara, Deus, Deus meus: quare tristis es, ánima mea, et quare contúrbas me?

S. Spera in Deo, / quóniam adhuc confitébor illi: salutáre vultus mei, / et Deus meus.

P. Glória Patri, et Fílio, et Spirítui Sancto.

S. Sicut erat in princípio et nunc, et semper, / et in sæcula sæculórum. Amen.

P. Introíbo ad altáre Dei.

S. Ad Deum qui lætíficat juventútem meam.

P. Adjutórium nostrum ✞ in nómine Dómini.

S. Qui fecit cælum et terram.

Note that a certain sadness overshadows THE PRIEST while he is praising God. THE PRIEST beholds Christ before the great sacrifice of Calvary. He hears Christ's prayer in the Garden: "My soul is sorrowful even unto death."

Christ's sadness is THE PRIEST'S sadness: "Why are thou sad, O my soul?" The altar is Mount Calvary and the Mass is the renewal, in an unbloody manner, of the Sacrifice of the Cross.

Judica Me — Psalm 42

Judge me, O God, and distinguish my cause from the nation that is not holy: deliver me from the unjust and deceitful man.

S. For Thou, O God, art my strength: why hast Thou cast me off? and why do I go sorrowful whilst the enemy afflicteth me?

P. Send forth Thy light and Thy truth: they have led me and brought me unto Thy holy hill, and into Thy tabernacle.

S. And I will go in unto the Altar of God: unto God, who giveth joy to my youth.

P. I will praise Thee upon the harp, O God, my God: why art thou sad, O my soul? and why dost thou disquiet me?

S. Hope thou in God, for I will yet praise Him: Who is the salvation of my countenance, and my God.

P. Glory be to the Father, and to the Son, and to the Holy Ghost.

S. As it was in the beginning, is now, and ever shall be, world without end. Amen.

P. I will go in unto the Altar of God.

S. Unto God Who giveth joy to my youth.

P. Our help ✝ is in the Name of the Lord.

S. Who hath made heaven and earth

Yet, he must go on. Why? Christ went to Calvary out of love for us sinners. THE PRIEST at Mass is this same Christ-- he goes in persona Christi to the ALTAR OF SACRIFICE (to God) on behalf of himself and us.

P. Confíteor Deo omnipoténti, etc. *(as below)*
S. Misereátur tui omnípotens Deus, / et
  dimíssis peccátis tuis, / perdúcat te ad vitam
  ætérnam.
P. Amen.

CONFÍTEOR Deo omnipoténti, / beátæ Mariæ
semper Vírgini, / beáto Michaéli Archángelo, /
beáto Joanni Baptístae, / sanctis Apóstolis Petro
et Paulo, / ómnibus Sanctis, et tibi, Pater: / quia
peccávi nimis cogitatióne, verbo et ópere: *(here
strike the breast three times)* / mea culpa, mea culpa,
mea máxima culpa. / Ideo precor beátam Maríam
semper Vírginem, / beátum Michaélem
Archángelum, / beátum Joánnem Baptístam, /
sanctos Apóstolos Petrum et Paulum, / omnes
Sanctos, et te, Pater, / oráre pro me ad Dóminum
Deum nostrum.

P. Misereátur vestri omnípotens Deus, et
  dimíssis peccátis vestris, perdúcat vos ad
  vitam ætérnam.
S. Amen.
P. Indulgéntiam, ✟ absolutiónem, et
  remissiónem peccatórum nostrórum tríbuat
  nobis omnípotens et miséricors Dóminus.
S. Amen.

After reciting psalm 42 THE PRIEST becomes aware of
his unworthiness. Confessing his sins and begging
forgiveness, he bows down in sorrow, and with a contrite heart
he says: "Confiteor Deo omnipotenti." "I confess to Almighty
God."

P. I confess to Almighty God, etc. *(as below)*
S. May Almighty God have mercy upon you, forgive you your sins, and bring you to life everlasting.

P. Amen.

I confess to Almighty God, to blessed Mary ever Virgin, to blessed Michael the Archangel, to blessed John the Baptist, to the holy Apostles Peter and Paul, to all the Saints, and to you, Father, that I have sinned exceedingly, in thought, word and deed: *(here strike breast three times)* through my fault, through my fault, through my most grievous fault. Therefore I beseech blessed Mary ever Virgin, blessed Michael the Archangel, blessed John the Baptist, the holy Apostles Peter and Paul, all the Saints, and you, Father, to pray to the Lord our God for me.

P. May Almighty God have mercy upon you, forgive you your sins, and bring you to life everlasting.
S. Amen.
P. May the Almighty and merciful God grant us pardon, ✝ absolution, and remission of our sins.
S. Amen.

THE PRIEST is SINNER even as he now acts in persona Christi. Here, he properly admits the awful truth--HE IS A SINNER.

P. Deus, tu convérsus vivificábis nos.
S. Et plebs tua lætábitur in te.
P. Osténde nobis, Dómine, misericórdiam tuam.
S. Et salutáre tuum da nobis.
P. Dómine, exáudi oratiónem meam.
S. Et clamor meus ad te véniat.
P. Dóminus vobíscum.
S. Et cum spíritu tuo.

After THE PRIEST has confessed his sins and sought the pardon of heaven, he is confident of the mercy of God. Then, THE PRIEST begins to say two verses of the eighty-fourth psalm.

He ascends to the ALTAR OF GOD. How is it "of God?" Whenever possible, God "in" the Eucharist is present before the altar as the One to Whom the Holy Sacrifice is offered.

The Catholic altar is indeed an awesome place. Each altar is sanctified by the relics of the saints, consecrated by the holy oils blessed by a bishop. Here is an altar--no mere table.

Here the Sacrifice of the Mass is celebrated. Here in the tabernacle dwells the Eucharistic Lord--GOD HIMSELF. "How terrible is this place! This is no other but the house of God, and the gate of heaven" (Gen. 28:17).

P. Thou wilt turn, O God, and bring us to life.
S. And Thy people shall rejoice in Thee.
P. Show us, O Lord, Thy mercy.
S. And grant us Thy salvation.
P. O Lord, hear my prayer.
S. And let my cry come unto Thee.
P. The Lord be with you.
S. And with thy spirit.

Europe's identity comes from its cathedrals--temples built for the Holy Sacrifice AND to more fittingly house or tabernacle Him Who deigns to remain with us for us to ADORE. Before Him, THE PRIEST "most fittingly" PRAYS HIS MASS.

The reigning upper clergy have expelled Jesus from His temples. The reigning upper clergy have forbidden the saying of that Mass which He formulated and His Church canonized.

As you attend Mass or, if you are a priest as you celebrate Mass, offer this, THE Sacrifice, in Reparation to the Two Sacred Hearts for modern liturgical sinful abuses and for other outrages against them. Console the loving Hearts of Jesus and Mary. They receive blasphemy; sacrilege and outrage even from the upper clergy of Christ's Church.

"The HOLY MASS is Calvary
all over again,
bridging the gap
of time and space,
and reaching us
after centuries of Holy Masses."

St. Peter Julian Eymard

GLÓRIA in excélsis Deo, / et in terra pax homínibus / bonæ voluntátis. / Laudámus te. / Benedícimus te. / Adorámus te. / Glorificámus te. / Grátias ágimus tibi / propter magnam glóriam tuam. / Dómine Deus, / Rex caeléstis, / Deus Pater omnípotens. / Dómine Fili unigénite, / Jesu Christe. / Dómine Deus, / Agnus Dei, / Fílius Patris. / Qui tollis peccáta mundi, / miserére nobis. / Qui tollis peccáta mundi, / súscipe deprecatiónem nostram. / Qui sedes ad déxteram Patris, / miserére nobis. / Quóniam tu solus Sanctus. / Tu solus Dóminus. / Tu solus Altíssimus, Jesu Christe. / Cum Sancto Spíritu, ✠ / in glória Dei Patris. / Amen.

Glory denotes that somebody's good is known and acknowledged. God demands that He become known to all men and that His attributes be known by all men, thereby also evoking adoration of God.

Glory be to God on high. And on earth peace to men of good will. We praise Thee. We bless Thee. We adore Thee. We glorify Thee. We give Thee thanks for Thy great glory. Lord God, heavenly King, God the Father Almighty. Lord Jesus Christ, Only-begotten Son, Lord God, Lamb of God, Son of the Father. Thou Who takest away the sins of the world, have mercy on us. Thou Who takest away the sins of the world, receive our prayer. Thou Who sittest at the right hand of the Father, have mercy on us. For Thou alone art holy. Thou alone art the Lord. Thou alone, O Jesus Christ, art most high. With the Holy Ghost, ✝ in the glory of God the Father. Amen.

With this prayer, adore God or rather prepare to devoutly participate in THE Saving-Event which alone allows us who are properly repentant sinners to give proper adoration to God.

THE ORATIONS

P. Dóminus vobíscum.   P. The Lord be with you.
S. Et cum spíritu tuo.   S. And with thy spirit.
                              P. Let us pray.

The COLLECT is a PROPER.

A PROPER changes with each Mass.

After the Gloria THE PRIEST turns toward the people and speaks the words which the archangel Gabriel, at the Annunciation, spoke: "Dominus vobiscum." "The Lord is with thee."

Then he reads the prayer, Oratio, of the Mass that states the mystery or the occasion for which this particular Mass is celebrated. The more ancient prayers particularly are remarkable for their beauty of language. The ancients were adept at symmetrical construction and rhythmical phrasing.

Orations are not merely private prayers of THE PRIEST as are other prayers of the Mass, but public or official prayers of the Church, prayers by which the Church addresses God and presents her petition for the welfare of Catholics. St. Thomas remarked: "Public prayer is that which is offered to God by the ministers of the Church representing the body of the faithful."

A priest is not an agent or a manager, or a presider or a facilitator. He is one whose very office is that of being a vicar or mediator between God and man and between man and God.

There is no mediatorship except by prayer. Here in the Mass, THE PRIEST exercises this office of mediator. He in persona Christi prays for the people; and gives Christ to the Catholic faithful--in words and foremost, in truth.

Since THE PRIEST alone celebrates Mass he alone in persona Christi prays FOR man and "most especially" prays THE SAVING-EVENT or THE MASS. Thus he brings to our here and now CHRIST FOR US. THE PRIEST is the BRIDGE between men and God and between God and men.

THE EPISTLE, THE GOSPEL AND THE SERMON

The GOSPEL changes with each Mass.
The EPISTLE changes with each Mass.

S. Deo gratias.   S. Thanks be to God.

The Epistle, as it were, prepares the way of the Lord. The Gospel is the Word of God as announced by Jesus Christ. It is read by THE PRIEST.

As the mission of Christ was to be Prophet, Priest and King, so we find in the Mass the threefold offices of the Saviour reflected in His priests' office. When THE PRIEST reads the Gospel and preaches, the mystical Christ re-enacts His office as Prophet and Teacher.

Christ came into this world to bring the manna of heavenly truth. Early in life, He left the barren grounds of the desert and "began to preach..." (Matt 4:17). He "went out through the whole country. And He taught in their synagogues..." (Luke 4:14-15).

Christ commissions each priest to preach. Each priest, in virtue of his ordination, is invested with the office of a preacher.

In the Mass he executes this office when he reads the Epistle and Gospel, and when he preaches. Hence the sermon is not an interruption of the Mass, but is part of the liturgy of THE PRIEST's Mass.

When THE PRIEST delivers the Word of God, he executes Christ's preaching mission. He acts as Christ to His flock.

CREDO in unum Deum, / Patrem omnipótentem, / factórem cæli et terræ, / visibílium ómnium et invisibílium. / Et in unum Dóminum Jesum Christum, / Fílium Dei unigénitum. / Et ex Patre natum / ante ómnia sæcula. / Deum de Deo, / lumen de lúmine, / Deum verum de Deo vero. / Génitum, non factum, / consubstantiálem Patri: / per quem ómnia facta sunt. / Qui propter nos hómines / et propter nostram salútem / descéndit de cælis. /   *(Here all kneel):*

ET INCARNÁTUS EST DE SPÍRITU SANCTO / EX MARÍA VÍRGINE: / ET HOMO FACTUS EST. *(rise)*

Crucifíxus étiam pro nobis: / sub Póntio Piláto / passus, et sepúltus est. / Et resurréxit tértia die, / secúndum Scriptúras. / Et ascéndit in cælum: / sedet ad déxteram Patris. / Et íterum ventúrus est cum glória / judicáre vivos et mórtuos: / cujus regni non erit finis. /

Et in Spíritum Sanctum, / Dóminum et vivificántem: / qui ex Patre, Filióque procédit. / Qui cum Patre, et Fílio / simul adorátur, / et conglorificátur: / qui locútus est per Prophétas./ Et unam, sanctam, cathólicam / et apostólicam Ecclésiam. / Confíteor unum baptísma / in remissiónem peccatórum. / Et expécto resurrectiónem mortuórum. / Et vitam ✞ ventúri sæculi. / Amen.

P. Dóminus vobíscum.
R. Et cum spíritu tuo.
P. Orémus

After the Gospel has been read the Creed is often said by THE PRIEST. This "I believe" focuses us on Reality.

I BELIEVE

I believe in one God, the Father Almighty, Creator of heaven and earth, and of all things visible and invisible. And in one Lord Jesus Christ, the Only-begotten Son of God. Born of the Father before all ages. God of God, Light of Light, true God of true God. Begotten, not made: consubstantial with the Father; by Whom all things were made. Who for.us men, and for our salvation, came down from heaven.   *(Here all kneel)*

AND WAS INCARNATE BY THE HOLY GHOST OF THE VIRGIN MARY: AND WAS MADE MAN. *(rise)*

He was crucified also for us, suffered under Pontius Pilate, and was buried. And on the third day He rose again according to the Scriptures. And He ascended into heaven, and sitteth at the right hand of the Father. And He shall come again with glory to judge the living and the dead: of Whose kingdom there shall be no end.

And I believe in the Holy Ghost, the Lord and Giver of Life: Who proceedeth from the Father and the Son. Who together with the Father and the Son is adored and glorified: Who spoke through the Prophets. And in One, Holy, Catholic and Apostolic Church, I confess one Baptism for the remission of sins. And I look for the resurrection of the dead, and the life ✝ of the world to come. Amen.

P. The Lord be with you.
S. And with thy spirit.
P. Let us pray.

Here in the creed is contained a summation of some of the God-given Realities or basic tenets in which EACH ONE is called to believe. "WE believe" implies an unreal abstraction. Each believes or doesn't believe.

"In the HOLY MASS are contained
all the fruits, all the graces,
all those immense treasures
which the Son of God
poured out so abundantly
upon the Church."

St. Thomas

MASS OF THE FAITHFUL

NOTE: Wherever a PROPER is given for that particular day,
we will cite an appropriate Mass prayer for you to pray
and contemplate.

THE OFFERTORY

The OFFERTORY is a PROPER.

A PROPER changes with each Mass.

SÚSCIPE, sancte Pater, omnípotens æterne Deus, hanc immaculátam hóstiam, quam ego indignus fámulus tuus óffero tibi Deo meo vivo et vero, pro innumerabílibus peccátis, et offensiónibus, et negligéntiis meis, et pro ómnibus circumstántibus, sed et pro ómnibus fidélibus christiánis vivis atque defúnctis: ut mihi et illis profíciat ad salútem in vitam ætérnam. Amen.

Recall that THE PRIEST in persona Christi offers Christ, NOT bread or wine. "'To what purpose do you offer Me the multitude of your victims?' saith the Lord. I desire not holocausts of rams, and fat of fatlings and blood of calves and lambs and buck goats" (Isa 1:11). God has NO need of bread and wine.

"HANC IMMACULATAM HOSTIAM"--this Spotless Victim, Christ--is offered to God present in the tabernacle. NOTHING ELSE IS ACCEPTABLE TO GOD.

THE OFFERTORY

The OFFERTORY is a PROPER.

A PROPER changes with each Mass.

Accept, O Holy Father, Almighty and Everlasting God, this unspotted Host, which I, Thine unworthy servant, offer unto Thee, my living and true God, to atone for my countless sins, offenses, and negligences: on behalf of all here present and likewise for all faithful Christians, living and dead, that it may avail both me and them as a means of salvation, unto life everlasting. Amen.

WHY did Christ become man? Why Calvary? Why each Mass? To bring each properly disposed person "ad salutem in vitam aeternam"--to salvation "into" eternity.

Be inspired to realize that your four essential obligations to God can hereby be fulfilled--adore God, obtain reparation or justification, thank God; and petition for others. Be devout. Increase your devotion.

DEUS, ✠ qui humánae substántiae dignitátem mirabíliter condidísti et mirabílius reformásti: da nobis, per hujus aquæ et vini mystérium, ejus divinitátis esse consórtes, qui humanitátis nostræ fíeri dignátus est párticeps, Jesus Christus, Fílius tuus, Dóminus noster: Qui tecum vivit et regnat in unitáte Spíritus Sancti Deus: per omnia sæcula sæculórum. Amen.

THE PRIEST now goes to the Epistle side where he pours wine and after blessing the water, pours water also into the chalice. What is the significance of mingling water with wine and why does THE PRIEST not bless the wine, whereas he blesses the water?

"Water," says St. Thomas, "ought to be mingled with the wine which is offered in this sacrament. First of all on account of its institution, for it is believed that our Lord instituted this sacrament in wine tempered with water according to the custom of that country (Prov 9:5). Secondly because it harmonizes with the representation of our Lord's Passion. Hence Pope Alexander I says: 'In the Lord's chalice neither wine only nor water only ought to be offered, but both mixed because we read that both flowed from His side in the Passion'" (Summa theol., IIIa, q.74. a.6).

O God, ✟ Who in creating man didst exalt his nature very wonderfully and yet more wonderfully didst establish it anew; by the Mystery signified in the mingling of this water and wine, grant us to have part in the Godhead of Him Who hath deigned to become a partaker of our human- ity, Jesus Christ, Thy Son, our Lord; Who liveth and reigneth with Thee, in the unity of the Holy Ghost, God. World without end. Amen.

The shedding of the blood belonged directly to Christ's Passion; for it is natural for blood to flow from a wounded human body. But the flowing of the water was not necessary for the Passion; but merely to show its effect, which is to wash away sins and to refresh us from the heat of concupiscence. (Ibid.)

Third, because this is adapted for signifying the effect of this sacrament, since as Pope Julius says: "We see that the faithful are signified by the water, but Christ's blood by the wine. Therefore when water is mixed with the wine in the chalice, the faithful are made one with Christ" (Concil. Bracarens, III, canon 1.) and (Summa theol., IIIa, q.74. a.6).

"The best method of PARTICIPATING
in the Holy Sacrifice of the Mass
is to unite oneself with the august Victim.

United to the offering of Jesus Christ,
your offering will be ennobled, purified,
made worthy of God's attention.

Follow Jesus Christ to Calvary,
meditating on the events
of His Passion and Death."

St. Peter Julian Eymard

OFFÉRIMUS tibi, Dómine, cálicem salutáris, tuam deprecántes cleméntiam: ut in conspéctu divínæ majestátis tuæ, pro nostra et totíus mundi salúte, cum odóre suavitátis ascéndat. Amen.

The renowned Doctor, St. Albert the Great in his Treatise on the Sacrifice of the Mass, insists that the external oblation ought to be a sign of our interior offering. He wrote: "The assembly does not merely offer material gifts: he who offers a gift at the same time offers himself to THE PRIEST that he may himself be offered to God."

"OFFERIMUS... CALICEM SALUTARIS..." Christ, as it were, extends HIS prerogative as offerer and the offering to US--as much as this is possible.

Are laymen then equal to priests? MOST CERTAINLY NOT; nor are laymen Christ's equal. Only consumately proud New Age "Catholics" dare think or utter such "blasphemous sacrilege."

We offer unto Thee, O Lord, the chalice of salvation, entreating Thy mercy that our offering may ascend with a sweet fragrance in the sight of Thy divine Majesty, for our own salvation, and for that of the whole world. Amen.

How then can and do "we offer?" We offer on the basis of the Colossians' mystery as expressed in Chapter one, verse twenty-four: "I make up what is lacking in the sufferings of Christ IN MY BODY, for the sake of His Body, the Church" (my faithful version of Col 1:24).

Whenever, and to the extent that Christ lives in any human soul THIS side of death, He does so TO SUFFER AND TO DIE. That's the "Christ-force" as experienced by or "in" any "pre-death" human being.

Christ, living in any Catholic, makes that Catholic an Offerer and an Offered to God the Father. Thus Christ makes such Catholics "part of each Mass." Each offers and is offered.

IN spíritu humilitátis, et in ánimo contríto suscipiámur a te, Dómine: et sic fiat sacrifícium nostrum in conspéctu tuo hódie, ut pláceat tibi, Dómine Deus.

VENI, Sanctificátor omnípotens ætérne Deus: et bené dic ✠ hoc sacrifícium, tuo sancto nómini præparátum.

Thus you united to Christ offer Christ and are united to Christ as offering or as offered. The ONLY offering and offered acceptable to God are THE MASS.

Therefore YOU as being willingly offered with Christ; as willingly offering Christ in you (the only hope of glory); and as living not you but Christ in YOU can offer Christ and be offered as Christ-Victim.

What an infinitely great extension of grace and mercy! Pause; realize this great truth; live it; thank God for it; and see its PRIME Source, Sustenance; and Realization or Summit in each valid Mass (offered properly by a validly ordained priest).

Humbled in spirit and contrite of heart, may we find favor with Thee, O Lord: and may our sacrifice be so offered this day in Thy sight as to be pleasing to Thee, O Lord God.

Come Thou, the Sanctifier, Almighty and Everlasting God, and bless ✝ this sacrifice which is prepared for the glory of Thy holy Name.

YOU do not celebrate Mass. YOU, unless you are a priest, CANNOT celebrate Mass. However, at each Mass, each one who desires and lives Christ SOMEHOW participates IN CHRIST as offering and as offerer. Be content. Don't be a proud NOELITE who in boldly claiming to celebrate Mass brings down God's wrath.

One last note is to be pondered. YOU, as in the state of Sanctifying Grace and AS devoutly attending Mass CAN, in CHRIST, make supplication for the "poor" souls--those in Purgatory (those in Hell cannot be helped by our prayers). Remember them. They are in great need of fraternal love.

Also, as "devoutly graced" remember to pray for yourself and for "yours." Pray for REAL needs--salvation from eternal Hell; sanctification; and a lessening of the pains of Purgatory.

AT THE LAVABO
OR
THE WASHING OF THE FINGERS

O WHAT cleanness and purity of heart
ought we to bring with us
to this great sacrifice!

BUT ALAS! I am a poor unclean sinner.

O WASH ME, dear Lord
from all stains of sin
in the blood of the Lamb,
that I may be worthy to be present
at these heavenly mysteries.

O MOST HOLY and ADORABLE TRINITY,
vouchsafe to help each of us
to die to our sins,
to die with Christ
in order to live with Him.

LAVÁBO inter innocéntes manus meas: et circúmdabo aitáre tuum, Dómine. Ut áudiam vocem laudis: et enárrem univérsa mirabília tua. Dómine, diléxi decórem domus tuæ: et locum habitatiónis glóriæ tuæ. Ne perdas cum ímpiis, Deus: ánimam meam, et cum viris sánguinum vitam meam. In quorum mánibus iniquitátes sunt: déxtera eórum repléta est munéribus.

Ego autem in innocéntia mea ingréssus sum: rédime me, et miserére mei. Pes meus stetit in dirécto: in ecclésiis benedícam te, Dómine.

Glória Patri, et Fílio, et Spirítui Sancto. Sicut erat in princípio, et nunc, et semper, et in sæcula sæculórum. Amen.

Now, as it were, we re-focus on THE Sacrifice--that of Christ on our behalf. To "perform" this sacrifice more fruitfully, THE PRIEST should be free from sins. Symbolically, he washes his hands. However, his prayers show him and us that nothing less than real purity of soul should be his and ours. God's Sacrifice demands our sacrificial cooperation. Luther's heresy, of God covering over all sinfulness because of Christ, is just that--HERESY.

I will wash my hands among the innocent, and I will encompass Thine Altar, O Lord. That I may hear the voice of praise, and tell of all Thy wondrous works. I have loved, O Lord, the beauty of Thy house, and the place where Thy glory dwelleth. Take not away my soul, O God, with the wicked, nor my life with men of blood. In whose hands are iniquities, their right hand is filled with gifts.

But as for me, I have walked in my innocence; redeem me, and have mercy on me. My foot hath stood in the right way; in the churches I will bless Thee, O Lord.

Glory be to the Father, and to the Son, and to the Holy Ghost. As it was in the beginning, is now, and ever shall be, world without end. Amen.

Recall at this time the spiritual meaning of the washing of the fingers. "This action," wrote St. Cyril of Jerusalem, "shows that THE PRIEST must be free from all sin. It is his hands which have done these things; to wash his hands is the nearest thing to purifying his deeds." Referring to Pontius Pilate's action before condemning Jesus to crucifixion, a religious author wrote "Let us take good care that each one of us can say in all truth 'I am innocent of the Blood of Jesus Christ.'"

PRAYER TO MOST HOLY TRINITY

SÚSCIPE, sancta Trínitas, hanc oblatiónem, quam tibi offérimus ob memóriam passiónis, resurrectiónis, et ascensiónis Jesu Christi Dómini nostri, et in honórem beatæ Mariae semper Vírginis, et beáti Joánnis Baptístæ, et sanctórum Apostolórum Petri et Pauli, et istórum, et ómnium Sanctórum: ut illis profíciat ad honórem, nobis autem ad salútem: et illi pro nobis intercédere dignéntur in cælis, quorum memóriam ágimus in terris. Per eúmdem Christum Dóminum nostrum. Amen.

Why are we here? "Ad salutem"--for salvation. There is no place in the official and canonized Mass for these banal and silly petitions which pervade NOEL's celebrations by MAN and for MAN.

PRAYER TO MOST HOLY TRINITY

Receive, O Holy Trinity, this oblation which we make to Thee in memory of the Passion, Resurrection and Ascension of our Lord Jesus Christ; and in honour of Blessed Mary ever Virgin, of blessed John the Baptist, the holy Apostles Peter and Paul, of these and of all the Saints. To them let it bring honor, and to us salvation, and may they whom we are commemorating here on earth deign to plead for us in heaven. Through the same Christ our Lord. Amen.

Orate Fratres

ORÁTE, fratres: ut meum ac vestrum sacrifícium acceptábile fiat apud Deum Patrem omnipoténtem.

S. Suscípiat Dóminus sacrifícium de mánibus tuis / ad laudem et glóriam nóminis sui, / ad utilitátem quoque nostram, / totiúsque Ecclésiæ suæ sanctæ.

P. Amen.

How is the Mass OUR sacrifice? In as much as Christ lives in you and you live, not you but Christ in you, Christ will be CRUCIFIED as you die to your flesh (your own body and mind in their natural desires) and to the world (living for/from other humans).

Orate Fratres

Pray, brethren, that my Sacrifice and yours may be acceptable to God the Father Almighty.

S. May the Lord accept the Sacrifice from thy hands, to the praise and glory of His Name, for our benefit and for that of all His holy Church.

P. Amen.

As CRUCIFIED THROUGH, WITH and IN CHRIST you are offered to the Heavenly Father. "Your" sacrifice is acceptable only to the extent it is CHRIST'S SACRIFICE or to the extent that you are dead to your flesh and the world and alive ONLY to Christ's will in you.

"If we had faith, we should see
the heavenly host gathered around
the Altar during Mass
since it is undoubted that
the whole heavenly court is then present."

Council of Oxford
Anno 1222

THE SECRET(S)

The SECRET is a PROPER.

THE PREFACE

P. Per ómnia sæcula sæculórum.
S. Amen.
P. Dóminus vobíscum.
S. Et cum spíritu tuo.
P. Sursum corda.
R. Habémus ad Dóminum.
P. Grátias agámus Dómino Deo nostro.
R. Dignum et justum est.

Preface

VERE dignum et justum est, æquum et salutáre, nos tibi semper et ubíque grátias ágere: Dómine, sancte Pater, omnípotens ætérne Deus: Qui cum unigénito Filio tuo, et Spíritu Sancto, unus es Deus, unus es Dóminus: non in uníus singularitáte persónæ, sed in uníus Trinitáte substántiæ. Quod enim de tua glória, reveláte te, crédimus, hoc de Fílio tuo, hoc de Spíritu Sancto, sine differéntia discretiónis sentímus. Ut in confessióne veræ sempiternæque Deitátis, et in persónis propríetas, et in esséntia únitas, et in majestáte adorétur æquálitas. Quam laudant Angeli atque Archángeli, Chérubim quoque ac Séraphim: qui non cessant clamáre quotídie, una voce dicéntes:

The Canonized Mass gives proper adoration to God. Jesus Christ offers up Himself to the honor and glory of His heavenly Father. The Church, by the Sacrifice of the Mass, renders to the Almighty the praise and adoration that Catholics owe to God.

106

THE SECRET(S)

A PROPER changes with each Mass.

THE PREFACE

P. World without end.
S. Amen.
P. The Lord be with you.
S. And with thy spirit.
P. Lift up your hearts.
S. We have lifted them up to the Lord.
P. Let us give thanks to the Lord our God.
S. It is right and just.

Preface (Of the Most Holy Trinity)

It is truly meet and just, right and profitable for our salvation, that we should at all times and in all places, give thanks unto Thee, O holy Lord, Father Almighty, Everlasting God; Who, together with Thine Only-begotten Son, and the Holy Ghost, art one God, one Lord; not in the oneness of a single Person, but in the Trinity of one substance. For what we believe by Thy revelation of Thy glory, the same do we believe of Thy Son, the same of the Holy Ghost, without difference or inequality. So that in confessing the True and Everlasting Godhead, distinction in Persons, unity in Essence, and equality in Majesty may be adored. Which the Angels and Archangels, the Cherubim also and the Seraphim do praise: who cease not daily to cry out, with one voice saying:

God is the source, "sustainer" and goal of the Canonized Mass. MAN is at best a repentant SINNER. As a sinner MAN can give nothing to God. Liturgy as a work of MAN as claimed by NOEL (Novus Ordo English Liturgy) is VAIN. GOD ALONE IS HOLY.

Sanctus, Sanctus, Sanctus, Dóminus Deus Sábaoth. Pleni sunt cæli, et terra glória tua. Hosánna in excélsis.

✟ Benedíctus qui venit in nómine Dómini. Hósanna in excélsis.

St. Thomas points out the two-fold aspect of this prayer, when he says "The priest and the people devoutly praise Christ's Godhead, saying with the angels: 'Holy, Holy, Holy; and His humanity, saying with the children: Blessed is He that comes'" (Summa theol., IIIa, q.83, a.4).

Holy, Holy, Holy, Lord God of Hosts. Heaven and earth are full of Thy Glory. Hosanna in the highest.

✟ Blessed is He who cometh in the Name of the Lord. Hosanna in the highest.

The "Sanctus" reminds us that since THE PRIEST's Prayer of the Mass is Christ's Prayer, it brings us into Heaven even as it brings Heaven to us.

OFFERTORY

"At <u>my</u> Holy Mass,
I never tire of standing so long.

I am not standing
but am on the cross with Christ
suffering with Him."

Padre Pio

Canon

TE ígitur, clementíssime Pater, per Jesum Christum Fílium tuum, Dóminum nostrum, súpplices rogámus, ac pétimus, uti accépta hábeas, et benedícas, hæc ✟ dona, hæc ✟ múnera, hæc ✟ sancta sacrifícia illibáta, in primis, quæ tibi offérimus pro Ecclésia tua sancta cathólica: quam pacificáre, custodíre, adunáre, et régere dignéris toto orbe terrárum: una cum fámulo tuo Papa nostro N. . . et Antístite nostro N. . . et ómnibus orthodóxis, atque cathólicæ et apostólicæ fídei cultóribus.

After THE PRIEST has finished the triumphant Preface and glorified God in the Sanctus, he enters into HIS silent prayers of the Canon. His first thought is to ask God "the most merciful Father" to "accept" and "bless" the Sacrifice of the Mass.

Why? This Mass is HIS, THE PRIEST'S Mass, and as such needs to be blessed "into propriety" and "out of any impropriety." So THE PRIEST prays that God may accept and bless His Mass (accepta habeas et benedictas).

"TE IGITUR..."

Now the celebrant, as Christ, addresses the most merciful Father, to beseech him to accept these oblations and bless them. "Bless" has God as its subject. It means God gives us a token of His benevolence. The most merciful Father can only "accept and bless" since these gifts, these offerings are the holy and unblemished Sacrifice--Christ's Body and Blood.

FOR THE CHURCH

We, therefore, humbly pray and beseech Thee, most merciful Father, through Jesus Christ Thy Son, Our Lord, to accept and to bless these ✞ gifts, these ✞ presents, these ✞ holy unspotted Sacrifices, which we offer up to Thee, in the first place, for Thy Holy Catholic Church, that it may please Thee to grant her peace, to preserve, unite, and govern her throughout the world; as also for Thy servant N. . . our Pope, and N. . . our Bishop, and for all orthodox believers and all who profess the Catholic and Apostolic faith.

Haec dona are these gifts which God has given FOR man and which THE PRIEST offers as "gifts" to God. Haec munera--Christ's Sacrifice is freely given to us through THE PRIEST. "It" is an unblemished offering--hanc sancta sacrificia illibata, the Body and Blood of Christ.

This particular Mass must be prayed to be "acceptable to God" since it is THE PRIEST's sacrifice. Either he prays properly; or he fails to pray properly.

The validly ordained priest "MAKES OR BREAKS" HIS Mass. Also, THE PRIEST's failure to use proper matter or to say the words (FORM) as the Catholic Church has canonized them to be said--any of these will invalidate HIS Mass.

Perhaps someday the Apocalypse will materialize (ch. 13). Sacrifice will cease. Only DECEPTION will prevail. Phony invalid Masses may one day cover the entire earth.

"WHAT" is "prayed and blessed" to be as God desires? These "givens" (dona), these "freely bestowed" (munera); and this "most holy offered sacrifice" (haec sancta sacrificia illibata)--Christ's Sacrifice.

Man cannot endure too much Reality at once. He must be led from "the given" to THE Sacrifice.

Masses are offered that the MEDIUM or BEARER of such gifts may always be faithfully such. May the establishment Church NEVER fail to be AS God demands it to be.

God will never desert His Church; BUT as the Apocalypse clearly discloses, not every establishment church IS Christ's church (cf. Rv 2;3). Always the Remnant will be Catholic. This Church will never cease to be. Make sure you are in THE Remnant.

Let's now look at a deeper meaning of the "TE IGITUR." As it were, let's take God's view of the Mass.

"TE, igitur"--THE PRIEST's prayer, the Mass, is approaching a climax. THE PRIEST as Christ addresses the Heavenly Father.

THE PRIEST-as-CHRIST--and yet at the same time realizing he is a weak human instrument--also beseeches the Heavenly Father to accept and bless THE offering as beneficial to us or as effective unto our salvation from Hell.

He, THE PRIEST, recalls himself. He in persona Christi is offering THE HOLY AND UNBLEMISHED SACRIFICE. Here is eternity--always praising the Lamb that is now being slain (Rev 5:13). Here, Heaven breaks into our own space and time THROUGH THE PRIEST and ONLY through THE PRIEST.

Indeed, HERE is THE gift (haec dona); HERE is the FREELY BESTOWED gift (haec munera). No human can claim a RIGHT to the Mass as the EFFECTIVE agent of his own salvation. "Haec sancta sacrificia illibata"--the infinitely

114

awesome and adorable Lamb now once again, IS SLAIN (in as much as God can repeat Calvary in our space and time) to attain eternal Heaven for Christ's ELECT.

The Mass IS freely given by Christ since the Mass is the effective Sacrifice of Calvary--effective ONLY for Christ's ELECT. HERE at each Mass, we can somehow say that HEAVEN (the souls of the faithful-departed) comes to earth. Resolve to make this SIGN of your election SURE by living as Christ demands.

The "Te igitur" is so powerful that its contents are explained or elaborated upon in the next three priest-prayers (Memento...Communicantes...Hanc Igitur).

Before we go on, let's prayerfully consider the remaining or last part of the "Te igitur." Here is contained the given Church-intention for this priest-Mass.

In the first place prayer is offered for the universal Catholic Church--semper et ubique. And here once again a blow is struck against religious individualism, which is not Catholic. When in the course of the Valerian Persecution, St. Fructeosus, the Bishop of Tarragona, was going to the stake, a certain Catholic commended himself to him: "Father, pray for me." The bishop answered "It is fitting that I should pray for the whole Catholic Church, spread out from East to West" (Ephes v, 25).

This is almost the wording of our Canon. Notice the word "thy" which in a way obliges God to grant what we ask. We are His Church. The Mass Prayer is offered that God will be pleased to give His Catholic Existential Church peace, to preserve her and to keep and guide her in unity throughout the whole world.

Let us ponder each of these four verbs. They express the constant needs of the Existential Church. The Church needs peace. Pacificare. The Mass-Prayer is offered that the Apostles' successors not forget the Saviour's command: that the Gospel must be preached unto all nations, to the uttermost parts of the earth, toto orbe terrarum. We seek peace throughout the world.

The first generations of Catholics sought peace but for two and a half centuries "persecution never completely ceased in the vast expanse of the Empire; it only died down here in order to spring to life again a little way away" (G. Boissier, La fin du paganisme, vol. I,p.347).

Now though persecution is one of those marks by which Jesus has said that men may know his Church and though it is a providential means of purification for Christians, it does not facilitate conversions. The Church therefore asks God to grant her peace, so that the spreading of the Gospel may be continued.

Custodire. External peace is not her greatest good. Then the Mass-Prayer is offered so that God may protect the existential Catholic Church against the dangers which she encounters in our day.

Adunare--may the whole existential Catholic Church and ALL of its parts be united with the ESSENTIAL Catholic Church, SEMPER ET UBIQUE (always and everywhere). Prayer is offered that the Church be strengthened against enemies from without and from within (custodire). How very needed is CL (the Canonized Liturgy) in this time of grave internal apostasy.

Finally pray that the Church be governed by the upper clergy AS God demands (regere). Each pope, each bishop and each priest, as also each Catholic, is EQUALLY BOUND by all of the official and binding teachings of the Catholic Faith. NOW especially, do we pray that the existential Catholic Church in EACH of its "parts" be ruled or governed according to the letter and spirit of these "semper et ubique held as binding" Catholic Dogmas, Beliefs and Practices.

One of the last things that Padre Pio did was
to write a letter to Pope Paul VI in which he said:

"I offer you my prayers and daily sufferings as
a small but sincere contribution on the part of the
least of your sons, in order that God may lead you
with His grace to follow the straight and painful
way in defense of eternal truth, which does not
change with the passing of the years."

Ten days later, the only priest-stigmatist in
The Church's history, died. Join him in praying for
the Pope that he may follow the straight and painful
path in defense of eternal truth--especially, the
eternal liturgized truth of the Canonized Mass.

MEMÉNTO, Dómine, famulórum famularúmque tuárum N. . . et N. . . et ómnium circumstántium, quorum tibi fides cógnita est, et nota devótio, pro quibus tibi offérimus: vel qui tibi ófferunt hoc sacrifícium laudis, pro se, suísque ómnibus: pro redemptióne animárum suárum, pro spe salútis et incolumitátis suæ: tibíque reddunt vota sua ætérno Deo, vivo et vero.

In the preceding prayer of the "Te igitur," THE PRIEST asks for the welfare of the Church and for each one's true welfare. This is the intention of Christ and of His Church. In the "Memento," THE PRIEST says HIS Mass for whomever he chooses.

Be mindful, O Lord, of Thy servants and hand-maids N. . . and N. . . and of all here present, whose faith and devotion are known to Thee, for whom we offer, or who offer up to Thee this Sacrifice of praise for themselves and all those dear to them, for the redemption of their souls and the hope of their safety and salvation: who now pay their vows to Thee, the everlasting, living and true God.

For WHAT does he pray? For the redemption of souls from Hell--not for banal and sensate pleasures. Also, he prays for that which will not impair the salvation of those for whom THE PRIEST prays--INCOLUMITATIS SUAE.

NEVER is THE Saving-Prayer to be trivialized and trashed into being a prayer for our "sensual desires." Such praying invites God's wrath.

COMMUNICÁNTES, et memóriam venerántes, in primis gloriósae semper Vírginis Maríæ, Genitrícis Dei et Dómini nostri Jesu Christi: sed beatórum Apostolórum ac Mártyrum tuórum, Petri et Pauli, Andréæ, Jacóbi, Joánnis, Thomæ, Jacóbi, Philíppi, Bartholomæi, Matthæi, Simónis et Thaddæi: Lini, Cleti, Cleméntis, Xysti, Cornélii, Cypriáni, Lauréntii, Chrysógoni, Joánnis et Pauli, Cosmæ et Damiáni: et ómnium Sanctórum tuórum; quorum méritis precibúsque concédas, ut in ómnibus protectiónis tuæ muniámur auxílio. Per eúmdem Christum Dóminum nostrum. Amen.

As the Apocalypse states--our glory will be praising the Lamb that was slain. The Mass is the LIFE OF HEAVEN. The slain Lamb, Christ Sacrificed, is the Focal Point of Heaven; and thus the focal point of each valid Mass.

INVOCATION OF THE SAINTS

In communion with, and honoring the memory in the first place of the glorious ever Virgin Mary Mother of our God and Lord Jesus Christ; also of blessed Apostles and Martyrs, Peter and Paul, Andrew, James, John, Thomas, James, Philip, Bartholomew, Matthew, Simon and Thaddeus, Linus, Cletus, Clement, Sixtus, Cornelius, Cyprian, Lawrence, Chrysogonus, John and Paul, Cosmas and Damien, and of all Thy Saints. Grant for the sake of their merits and prayers that in all things we may be guarded and helped by Thy protection. Through the same Christ our Lord. Amen.

How very fitting is it to recall the saints--especially your favorite saints. They are here at Mass since the Saving-Person IS Heaven.

HANC ígitur oblatiónem servitútis nostræ, sed et cunctæ famíliæ tuæ, quæsumus, Dómine, ut placátus accípias: diésque nostros in tua pace dispónas, atque ab ætérna damnatióne nos éripi, et in electórum tuórum júbeas grege numerári. Per Christum Dóminum nostrum. Amen.

Again we are reminded of our one and only pressing necessity--to be justified unto eternal salvation from Hell. THIS is why we are here. Here is our Salvation. Here is THE Sacrifice from which all graces flow.

OBLATION OF THE VICTIM TO GOD

We beseech Thee, O Lord, graciously to accept this oblation of our service and that of Thy whole household. Order our days in Thy peace, and command that we be rescued from eternal damnation and numbered in the flock of Thine Elect. Through Christ our Lord. Amen.

Let us be most devoutly thankful. Here we are present to our only (potential) salvation from eternal Hell. Pray. Ask Christ to save YOU from Hell.

"WHY DO YOU SUFFER SO MUCH
AT THE CONSECRATION OF THE HOLY MASS?"

"These secrets are not revealed
without destroying them.

You ask me why I suffer.

I would like to weep torrents of tears.

Don't you comprehend the tremendous mystery?

GOD, VICTIM for our sins!

And PRIESTS are His butchers."

Padre Pio
Who NEVER said a Novus Ordo Mass

QUAM oblatiónem tu, Deus, in ómnibus, quæsumus, bene✝dictam, adscríp✝tam, ra✝tam, rationábilem, acceptabilémque fácere dignéris: ut nobis Cor✝pus, et San✝guis fiat dilectíssimi Fílii tui Dómini nostri Jesu Christi.

The prayer, "Quam oblationem," contains several words not easily comprehended and difficult to interpret, yet the general meaning of this prayer is easy to understand. But before we proceed to explain it, let us observe its peculiar position within the framework of the Canon.

Since entering into the sacred silence of the Canon, THE PRIEST has placed on the paten the prayers for the Church and the commemoration of the living. He has fortified himself with the thought that he does not stand alone at the altar, but is surrounded by the blessed and saints of Heaven, who come to his spiritual aid and support him by their prayers of intercession. And, finally, THE PRIEST has prayed for the blessings of peace, for his escape from eternal perdition and for his final salvation.

The awesome moment is at hand. The Consecration is about to take place. THE PRIEST will pronounce the very words that will effect the change of the bread and wine into the body and blood of our Lord Jesus Christ. To effect this most adorable Sacrament, THE PRIEST effects THE Sacrifice of Calvary. The Sacrament can only come to be through THE Sacrifice.

Humbly we pray Thee, O God, be pleased to make this same offering wholly blessed ✝ , to consecrate ✝ it and approve ✝ it, making it reasonable and acceptable, so that it may become for us the Body ✝ and Blood ✝ of Thy dearly beloved Son, our Lord Jesus Christ.

Therefore THE PRIEST prays most sincerely that THE (RITES OF THIS) OBLATION (oblationem) may be blessed (benedictam); done as prescribed by the canons of the Church (adscriptam); be ratified or accepted by God (ratam); and be "for sure and right now" THE ACCEPTABLE WAY (rationabilem acceptabilemque) TO BRING ABOUT THE SACRAMENT (ut nobis Corpus et Sanguis fiat Filii tui domini nostri Jesu Christi).

What care must be taken. As Pope Pius V canonically decreed. dare not anyone change in the least this Canon of the Mass. No one, not even a cardinal, can forbid THE PRIEST's saying the Canonized Mass--so decreed Saint Pius V.

In this time of pervasive internal apostasy, be thankful that YOU are attending the Canonized and binding Mass of the Roman Catholic Church. This Mass and these Mass Prayers go back to Apostolic times and were commanded by Christ-- so have our saints and reliable ancient authorities assured us and so has the Church spoken, by its officially and binding "canonizing" or making into THE RULE, these Mass prayers for its priests.

What a pity. What a shame. At the very time the Church needs the Mass and its graces IT forbids (in effect) its own Canonized Liturgy from being prayed. Pray for the pope. Pray for the Church.

CONSECRATION

"I SHOULD LIKE TO SHED TORRENTS OF TEARS
WHEN FACED WITH THE MYSTERY OF GOD-VICTIM.

We priests are the butchers of Jesus
during the Holy Mass,
while all of Paradise
reverently descends on the altar."

Padre Pio
Who said only the Tridentine (Canonized) Mass.

QUI prídie quam paterétur, accépit panem in sanctas ac venerábiles manus suas, et elevátis óculis in cælum ad te Deum Patrem suum omnipotentem, tibi grátias agens, bene✝dixit, fregit, dedítque discípulis suis, dicens: Accípite, et manducáte ex hoc omnes,

The Congregation is on its knees. THE PRIEST bends over the altar to re-enact what belongs entirely to the domain of faith. The great mystery of our holy religion, the Eucharistic Sacrifice, is being performed.

THE PRIEST's words change bread and wine into Christ's body and blood, for "... these words are uttered in the person of Christ" (Summa theol., IIIa, q.78, a.4). St. Thomas speaks, "Quasi ex persona ipsius Christi loquentis" (Ibid., a.1). As if Christ were speaking in person, THE PRIEST re-enacts the sacred proceedings that took place at Christ's first Mass.

He makes present again the hallowed events that took place previous to Christ's bitter Passion, for, when our Lord was about to ascend the altar of Calvary, He gave to His apostles His last and everlasting will. This Saving Will is THE PRIEST's will. It is the will which makes present again the Last Supper.

Who, the day before He suffered, took bread into His Holy and venerable hands, and having lifted up His eyes to heaven, to Thee, God, His Almighty Father, giving thanks to Thee, blessed it ✟, broke it, and gave it to His disciples, saying: Take and eat ye all of this,

The First Mass--realized at Calvary--is now made present once again. Christ is here. Christ offers Himself for our sins. Before this holiest of space-time moments materializes, we utter a thanksgiving to God for priests. ONLY priests are Christ. Only priests are Christ made present INTO our space-time to effect our salvation in THE mystery of faith--the Holy Sacrifice of the Mass.

The Lord "took bread into His holy and venerable hands." These sacred hands of the divine Master! In order that priests may perform this same act of the heavenly Lord, their hands were sacramentalized. They were especially anointed, blessed and prayed over by the bishop who ordained them. Saints and tradition assure us that our Lord, Himself, formulated the Canonized Liturgy. However, when we compare the words of the liturgical prayer "Qui pridie" with the report of the Last Supper scene, as given us by the Synoptics, do we not find that the words, "... into His holy and venerable hands, and with eyes lifted up towards heaven unto Thee, O God, His heavenly Father," are missing? To this the Angelic Doctor remarks:

"Our Lord said and did many things which are not written down by the Evangelists; and among them is the uplifting of His eyes to heaven at the supper; nevertheless the Roman Church had it by tradition from the apostles who obtained it from Christ. He who lifted up His eyes to the Father in raising Lazarus to life...in the prayer which He made for the disciples, has more reason to do so in instituting this Sacrament, as being of greater import" (Summa theol., IIIa, q.83, a.4, ad 2).

Christ--and THE PRIEST IN PERSONA CHRISTI-- lifting up His eyes, gave thanks to God His almighty Father. He thanked His heavenly Father that the great moment for the institution of the Sacrifice of the Mass, which he had so eagerly and lovingly longed for during His earthly life, was now at hand. He gave thanks to God that because of the establishment of this sacrifice and sacrament, He was to continue to dwell among men and be with them to the end of time--in sacrifice and in sacrament.

Only THE PRIEST speaks these words in the name of Christ. ONLY he is privileged to perform or re-do THE great Eucharistic offering. Only he is among us IN PERSONA CHRISTI.

THE PRIEST's "This is My body," effects the transubstantiation, that is, the conversion of the bread into the Body of Christ. To what does the pronoun "this" refer?

"These" words do not make the body of Christ to be the Body of Christ, nor do they make the bread to be the body of Christ. Expressly our Lord did not say: This bread is My body, ...nor This, My body is My body, ...but in general: This is My body, assigning no noun on the part of the subject, but only a pronoun, which signifies substance in common, without quality, that is, without a determinate form (St. Thomas, Summa throl. III). After each consecration comes the

132

elevation. Now, those attending Mass adore Christ. They adore "what appears to be bread"--WHO IS REALLY CHRIST.

Realize at this instance, Christ only came to be THE Sacrifice for your sins; and that Christ now comes ONLY as the "effect" or "fruit" of THE Unbloody Sacrifice. Adore Him. Thank Him for THE Saving Event.

Make an Act of Faith
in the REAL PRESENCE of your Saviour's
BODY, BLOOD, SOUL and DIVINITY
under the sacramental veils.

Offer yourself to Him
and through Him
to His Father.

Beg that your heart and soul
may be united to Him.

SÍMILI modo postquam cœnátum est, accípiens et hunc præclárum Cálicem in sanctas, ac venerábiles manus suas: item tibi grátias agens, bene✝dixit, deditque discípulis suis, dicens: Accípite, et bíbite ex eo omnes,

HIC EST ENIM CALIX SÁNGUINIS MEI,
NOVI ET ÆTERNI TESTAMÉNTI:
MYSTÉRIUM FIDEI:
QUI PRO VOBIS ET PRO MULTIS
EFFUNDÉTUR IN REMISSIÓNEM
PECCATÓRUM.

Haec quotiescúmque fecéritis, in mei memóriam faciétis.

MY LORD AND MY GOD!

CONSECRATION OF THE WINE

In like manner, after He had supped, taking also into His holy and venerable hands this goodly chalice, again giving thanks to Thee, He blessed it ✞, and gave it to His disciples, saying: Take and drink ye all of this:

FOR THIS IS THE CHALICE
OF MY BLOOD, OF THE NEW
AND EVERLASTING TESTAMENT:
THE MYSTERY OF FAITH:
WHICH SHALL BE SHED FOR YOU
AND FOR MANY
UNTO THE REMISSION OF SINS.

As often as ye shall do these things, ye shall do them in remembrance of Me.

MY LORD AND MY GOD!

THE ELEVATION

"We adore today," wrote St. Ambrose,
"Christ, Him Whom the Apostles adored."

St. Augustine wrote:
"Although we are not free from sin
when we adore,
not to adore
would be to sin."

After our Lord had pronounced the words of the Consecration, He said to His apostles: "Do this for a commemoration of Me" (Luke 22:19. Cf. I Cor. 11:24, 25).

Regarding this, St. Thomas makes the following remarks: "The power of consecrating this sacrament on Christ's behalf is bestowed upon the priest at his ordination, for thereby he is put upon a level with them to whom the Lord said, 'Do this for a commemoration of Me'" (Luke 22:19, Summa theol., IIIa, 9.82).

St. Thomas puts priests on the same level as the apostles. Every validly ordained priest is "equally" Christ among us as regards his God-given ability to re-present or make present for us THE Saving-Event, the Sacrifice of Calvary.

Each "CL-priest" is ordained to offer the Sacrifice of the Mass for the living and the dead. Each "NOEL-priest" EXPLICITLY is ordained as corroborator with the bishop AND to receive offertory gifts from people. WHY does NOEL endanger or invalidate Holy Orders? Pray for the pope!

PRAY THE HOLY MASS; PRAY GOOD FRIDAY; PRAY TO LIVE GOOD FRIDAY

Here is the HEART of the Mass. Here is the HEART of Good Friday. Here is YOUR inspiration and power to live YOUR Good Friday.

In Christ's Jewish calendar, our "Holy Thursday" IS REALLY the beginning of Good Friday. Thus, the First Mass and its "Bloody Realization" occurred on the same day-- GOOD FRIDAY. Each Mass brings GOOD FRIDAY to us.

Each Mass is Christ's Unbloody Sacrifice of Calvary--the HEART of Calvary made so present that Christ Himself becomes present to our space and time--Body, Blood, Soul and Divinity "under" the appearance of bread and wine. That which appears to be bread or wine IS NOW CHRIST HIMSELF. ADORE HIM MADE PRESENT BY THIS PRIEST-MASS.

Christ's Mass Prayer IS Christ's Good Friday Prayer or WILL. This was perfectly realized in the HUMAN NATURE of Christ--in His actual CRUCIFIXION.

MASS was perfectly realized in ONLY ONE HUMAN PERSON, the Blessed Mother, Mary. Such is to be realized IMPERFECTLY in each Catholic.

HERE is the HEART and the POWER of YOUR being crucified with Christ. Christ CRUCIFIED in YOU is your ONLY hope of glory.

Whenever Christ dwells in any true Catholic this side of death, He does so to enact or to complete Good Friday. Each is to be crucified to his own flesh (the natural desires or likings of his own estranged bodily appetites, thinking and desiring) and to his own world (to living for/from any one other than Christ or Mary who is the only human person "PERFECTLY TRANSPARENT TO GOD."

HERE, before you, is THE SALUTARY WILL (ACT) OF GOD--THAT WILL (ACT) WHICH CULMINATED IN THE BLOODY SACRIFICE BY WHICH YOU CAN BE OR ARE SAVED FROM HELL. Pray that Christ may be YOUR Saviour--now and eternally. Pray that the Holy Mass ACTUALLY BE FOR YOUR salvation.

Pray that for all eternity YOU may be a saved-sinner through the MASS and its bloody realization. Pray that THIS Holy Mass be EFFECTIVE UNTO YOUR SALVATION FROM HELL.

Also, HERE at this moment, pray that Christ's SALUTARY WILL may be in you to EFFECT YOUR Good Friday crucifixion. It is ONLY through Him, with Him and in

Him that YOU can render eternal "external" glory and honor to God for all eternity.

This, YOUR full realization, can ONLY come about THROUGH THE MASS. Pray the Holy Mass. Pray that the Holy Mass be EFFECTIVE IN YOUR EARTHLY LIFE UNTO YOUR CRUCIFIXION WITH CHRIST so that YOU may THUS come to reign with Him for all eternity.

ST. CHRYSOSTOM, in his writing on
THE PRIESTHOOD says:

"THE PRIEST is himself at that solemn moment
SURROUNDED BY ANGELS
and the choir of the heavenly powers unite with him;

they occupy the entire space around the altar,
to honor HIM who lies there
as THE sacrifice.

The angels are jubilant and triumphant--
since here on the altar
the most supreme act of worship and adoration
is rendered to God the Father.

In each HOLY MASS, the BODY and BLOOD
of His eternally Beloved Son
is offered up to the heavenly Father."

Gihr, THE HOLY SACRIFICE OF THE MASS
p. 662

"AS OFTEN AS YOU DO ALL OF THIS"

In the Bible, God teaches us that what WE do is useless at best and usually sinful. WE can do NOTHING without Christ.

AT BEST and at our best, we are INSTRUMENTS through which God acts. The instrument doesn't ACT. God ACTS. To Him ALONE belongs TOTAL WORSHIP (acknowledgement of TOTAL WORTH).

Here, at this "moment," is the ultimate expression or example of THIS GREAT TRUTH. According to the "NOEL-theoriticians" their presider does the DAMNABLE AND SACRILEGIOUS since he is merely one who is called from the community through their boss-bishop to be the boss-bishop's collaborator by presiding over the "people of God" in worship or by facilitating their own worship of God--from receiving their "GIFTS" to God...to NARRATING the Saving-Deed of Christ...to communing to each "person of God" by word and symbolism their own "Christedness."

"YOU ARE the Body of Christ"--so does NOEL (NOVUS ORDO ENGLISH LITURGY) assure each as individual and/or community. So does NOEL dethrone Christ to enthrone MAN as Christ.

On the other hand, WHO does "all of this" in the (CL) Canonized Liturgy? The ONE who does "all of this" ("HAEC") is and can only be a Christ-ordained priest who ALONE acts IN PERSONA CHRISTI. ONLY such a one can "haec facite"--"DO all of this"--no one else.

WHY? ONLY Christ saves and He saves ONLY AS HE DESIRES TO SAVE. He so loved us as to be present in His validly ordained priests--so present, that as they properly SAY Mass or "do all of this," they do so IN PERSONA CHRISTI, in His Own Person. As they act validly, Christ Himself ACTS salutarily.

At this solemn moment and throughout your days, thank God for "Christ among us"--His validly ordained priests who alone can, by their valid Masses, do "all of this," which brings to our own space and time both the Saving-Person, Christ, and His Saving-Deed, without Whom and without Which we are damned sinners.

CALICEM SALUTARIS

Again, we recall an apparent problem. The words or the form of the consecration of the chalice is not, in its entirety, reported by the Evangelists. St. Thomas Aquinas says that "the Evangelists did not intend to hand down the forms of the sacraments, which in the primitive Church had to be kept concealed...their object was to write the story of Christ." Divus Thomas continues:

Nevertheless nearly all these words can be culled from various passages of the Scriptures, because the words, "This...chalice," are found in Luke (Luke 22:20) and I Cor, (I Cor 11:25) and Matthew says, "This is My blood of the new testament, which shall be shed for many unto remission of sins" (Matt 26:28). The words added namely, "eternal" and "mystery of faith," were handed down to the Church by the Apostles who received them from Our Lord, according to I Cor, (I Cor 11:23) "I have received of the Lord that which also I delivered unto you" (Summa theol., IIIa, q. 78, a.3, ad 9).

The words or form of consecration of the wine come to us from Christ Himself. These are the words of the Canonized Mass.

Any deviation from these words invalidates the Mass for Roman Catholics of the Latin Rite. So teaches the Church-- directly and through its classical theologians.

145

More specifically and apropos of NOEL, anyone who can be convinced that "MULTIS" means "ALL" because the reigning experts and authorities dictate that it does--such a person has little or no hope of ever seeing and believing any natural truth and much less of coming to believe the TRUTHS that one must hold in order to be saved from Hell eternal.

Therefore, let's not waste too much time continually arguing with such MAN-worshippers. We are here to worship God. We are here to attend THE SACRIFICE OF THE MASS as prayed according to the Canonized Liturgy of the Catholic Church.

HERE is that which makes us CATHOLICS. HERE is that which liturgically defines the ONE AND ONLY CHURCH OF CHRIST, outside of which there is NO salvation.

Let's contemplate "THE POSITIVE OF GOD." Let's reject MAN and all of man's NEGATIVE death-oriented works and pomps.

HERE we have spelled out and REALIZED the calicem salutaris that WE IN CHRIST ARE offered to God. What does this chalice of our offertory "become" at the consecration of the Mass?

This chalice is really the chalice of Christ's Blood--of HIS sufferings, ONLY--and as much as--each Catholic is offered "as" or "in" Christ's chalice of suffering can he/she offer IN CHRIST, and NOT in persona Christi; nor, by himself, THE CHALICE OF SALVATION--calicem salutaris. Here is the apex of devotion for "Christ-sufferers."

Here again, we confront the Colossian Mystery (Co 1:24). Only those in Christ can and do offer the chalice of salvation to God. Only "Christ-sufferers" appreciate and adore Christ at Mass. Only "Christ-sufferers" can with true devotion attend Mass.

At the consecration, "Christ-sufferers" come into being IN CHRIST. Indeed, the Consecration--the Heart of each valid Mass--is the SOURCE OF; or gives meaning to; or enables truly faithful Catholics to offer the Chalice of salvation.

The chalice of salvation as understood by the Colossians' Mystery, is that which by Christ suffering in me fulfills what is lacking in the sufferings of Christ for His Body, the Church. SUCH suffering of Christ in me is salvific for myself and others.

AGENS ET DICENS

From Genesis to the Apocalypse, God ALWAYS comes to or encounters man AGENS ET DICENS--DOING AND SAYING. Why? God is alive.

God does. God says. Only then is man able to respond salutarily--unto his own individual salvation. Otherwise, man CANNOT enter Heaven. (Meditate on these truths).

The apex of the Real and Only Christ-Church--CHRIST AMONG US--is at the Consecration. Then, Christ-priest "agens..." and "dicens..." "GIVING thanks to His Heavenly Father... (He blessed and gave--SAYING "This is My Body (or Blood)..."

Ordinary alleged "people of God" or ordinary saved or unsaved MEN-individually or communally--CANNOT take CHRIST'S place. By, of and in itself, the community is NOTHING UNTO SALVATION. The Community CANNOT celebrate Mass.

ONLY Christ-priest--ONLY he who is validly empowered and validly acts and speaks IN PERSONA CHRISTI-- "effects" or "makes" CHRIST SO TO ACT AND SPEAK AMONG US AS TO HAVE CHRIST AND HIS SALUTARY ACT PRESENT TO THE CHRIST-PRIEST'S SPACE AND TIME. SO MUCH DOES CHRIST LOVE THAT HE HAS DEIGNED TO GIVE US CHRIST-PRIESTS.

Also, as Cardinal Ottaviani and other great authentic Catholic theologians have pointed out, TRUE Catholicism does NOT--as in protestant heretical and false rites and apparently as in NOEL--(Novus Ordo English Liturgy) narrate a PAST EVENT. True Catholicism through its Christ-priests "MAKES" CHRIST PRESENT AMONG US (as Vatican II correctly observed). ONLY when a Christ-priest is in persona Christi "agens et dicens," is there a VALID or TRUE Mass.

What NOEL proscribes, CL (Canonized Liturgy) prescribes. The Canonized Liturgy, in prescribed ritual deeds and words MAKES SURE, as best it can, that its Christ-priests "ACT" AND "DO" the Consecration.

"Giving thanks...saying..." ONLY then is the Mass VALID. Narration won't suffice.

Protestants who reject the Mass substitute a NARRATION. They seem to be content with NARRATING the Last Supper. If and when NOEL merely narrates, does it not ape Protestant services and SIMULATE the True Mass?

In a special way--after the Christ-priest "acts and says SALUTARILY"--RESPOND unto your salvation. Thank God "for Christ." Thank Christ. Petition Christ for your and others' salvation from Hell eternal. Praise. Believe. Adore. Love. Repent. Etc.

Bring the Consecration INTO the rest of your day, until the next valid Mass that you attend. Meditate on the Consecration for "IT" is YOUR ONLY salvation.

"To assist at HOLY MASS is supremely beneficial to us, because it means uniting ourselves with Jesus in His Holy Sacrifice.

There we receive the graces necessary for our repentance and justification, and aid against falling again into sin...

There we plead efficaciously the cause of the souls in Purgatory.

There we obtain the conversion of sinners.

There the saints find increase of external glory, and all heaven cause for rejoicing.

There, too, the answer to the question that human hearts in agony and pain have so often asked,

'Why must I suffer?'"

St. Peter Julian Eymard

UNDE et mémores, Dómine, nos servi tui, sed et plebs tua sancta, ejúsdem Christi Fílii tui Dómini nostri tam beátæ passiónis nec non et ab ínferis resurrectiónis, sed et in cælos gloriósæ ascensiónis: offérimus præclárae majestáti tuæ de tuis donis, ac datis, hóstiam ✟ puram, hóstiam ✟ sanctam, hóstiam ✟ immaculátam, Panem ✟ sanctum vitæ ætérnæ, et Cálicem ✟ salútis perpétuæ.

SUPRA quae propítio ac seréno vulta respícere dignéris: et accépta habére, sícuti accépta habére dignátus es munéra púeri tui justi Abel, et sacrifícium Patriárchæ nostri Abrahæ: et quod tibi óbtulit summus sacérdos tuus Melchísedech, sanctum sacrifícium, immaculátam hóstiam.

This prayer continues the previous one which emphasized the sacrificial character of the present sacred function. "Supra quae," by way of contrast emphasizes the magnificence and sublimity of the Eucharistic Sacrifice.

We do not offer sacrifices which are ineffective in themselves. We offer THE Sacrifice. However, since we sinners offer Christ and desire to be Christ's, we pray for a proper and profitable sacrificial attitude or devotion.

"UNDE ET MEMORES..."

So begins the first prayer immediately following the most solemn time of THE PRIEST'S Mass--the Consecration. "Unde et memores" are the first words of this august prayer.

And now, O Lord, we, Thy servants, and with us all Thy holy people, calling to mind the blessed Passion of this same Christ, Thy Son, our Lord, likewise His Resurrection from the grave, and also His glorious Ascension into heaven, do offer unto Thy most sovereign Majesty out of the gifts Thou hast bestowed upon us, the Victim ✟ Who is pure, the Victim ✟ Who is holy, the Victim ✟ Who is spotless, the holy Bread ✟ of life eternal, and the Chalice ✟ of everlasting Salvation.

Deign to look upon this with a favorable and gracious countenance, and to accept this as Thou didst accept the offerings of Thy just servant Abel, and the sacrifice of our Patriarch Abraham, and that which Thy high priest Melchisedech offered up to Thee, a holy sacrifice, an immaculate victim.

"UNDE"--Heaven which is defined by God in His Apocalypse as the "adoration of the Lamb that was slain (Apoc 5:11-14)" comes thence to us. Christ's ever-continuing (eternal) salvific WILL breaks into our space and time through a valid priest and his valid Mass. "UNDE" becomes Heaven Itself--the ADORABLE AND HEAVEN-DEFINING Unbloody Lamb-Slain.

"MEMORES"--Good Friday, the DAY of the FIRST MASS AND BLOODY SACRIFICE IS MADE PRESENT (as much as God can do so AT EACH VALID MASS). The Jewish day began at sunset on what we "wrongly" call Holy Thursday and ended on Good Friday--thus Christ's "Holy Thursday" Mass is REALLY His Good Friday Mass.

In these two prayers we are reminded that SACRIFICE is happening. We are here for SACRIFICE.

Briefly we recall the nature of SACRIFICE--the fact that conscious and enlightened sinners sought salvation and that some heard and obeyed God's "then-appointed" salvation plan. We recall Abel, Abraham and Melchisedech.

Abel is a type of Jesus by virtue of his obedience to God's will for sacrifice. The Lord looked with pleasure on the gifts he offered. The young shepherd's righteousness, however, unleashed the jealousy of his brother, Cain, and was the cause of his violent death, just as it was for envy that the Jewish authorities delivered up Jesus to Pilate.

Obeying God, Abraham offered Isaac, his only son, the subject of Divine promises, in sacrifice. The patriarch obeyed this harsh command, writes St. Paul, believing that God was able to raise his son from the dead (Heb xi, 17-19).

Melchisedech's sacrifice was a prefiguration of Christ's. Melchisedech was both King and Priest of the Most High. He did not hold his priesthood from his ancestors, as did the priests of Aaron; he held it by personal right, and his priesthood is eternal. Melchisedech is ageless; it is not known when he was born or when he died; thus he appears--always allegorically--to be outside time; a symbol of the Christ and of each of Christ's properly ordained priests, in the time after Calvary until the end of the world.

By the prayers of the Canon, THE PRIEST has been performing the most sacred act of religion, THE sacrifice. By the Consecration, under the two separated species of bread and wine, in the name and person of the Eternal High Priest, Jesus Christ, he has done the greatest act of worship, the all-holy sacrifice of the body and blood of the divine Victim, Jesus Christ.

The first prayer after the Consecration is a sacrificial prayer. The sacrificial gift (res oblata) is the pure, holy and immaculate Victim.

This prayer and the preceding words of the Consecration show that Christ acts through THE PRIEST. Here also, we have a reference to the Colossians' Mystery. WE are privileged to offer IN CHRIST the VICTIM (hostiam) Christ or the chalice of eternal salvation. Christ is THE SALUTARY VICTIM (hostiam sanctam...). It is the great privilege of Christ-sufferers to be offered with Christ and to offer Christ as victim--TO PRAY THE HOLY MASS.

"To me nothing is so consoling, so piercing,
so thrilling, so overcoming, as the HOLY MASS,
said as it is among us.
I could attend Masses forever and not be tired.

It is not a mere form of words--it is a great action,
THE GREATEST ACTION THAT CAN BE ON EARTH.

It is not the invocation merely but,
if I dare to use the word,
the EVOCATION of the Eternal.

HE becomes present on the altar in flesh and blood
before Whom angels bow and devils tremble.

That is that awful event which is the scope and
the interpretation of every part of the solemnity.

Words are necessary, but as means not as ends;
they are not mere addresses to the throne of grace,
they are instruments of what is far higher,
of consecration, of sacrifice."

Cardinal John Newman
on the Canonized Liturgy

"UNDE..." Heaven comes into our space and time. We are made present to Heaven. We call to mind the entire Saving Event--Christ's birth, life, passion and resurrection. Since Christ as RISEN is present, the Mass must be the effective Saving Deed.

Those who are saved, the elect of Christ, are present IN, TO and WITH the Resurrected Christ. They are His Mystical Body.

The MASS can never be the Saving Sacrifice "FOR ALL." SOME, NOT ALL, are actually saved and the MASS, as instituted by Christ and as solemnly, fully dogmatically, and bindingly defined by THE Church is THE EFFECTIVE SAVING DEED OF CHRIST.

"Memores..." emphasizes THE EFFECTIVE SAVING DEED. Christ is VICTIM or SACRIFICE for sin. GOOD FRIDAY is made present.

Christ is the pure VICTIM (hostiam puram); the ALL HOLY VICTIM (hostiam sanctam); and the totally sinless victim (hostiam immaculatam). This last phrase reminds us of the one only IMMACULATE HUMAN PERSON.

God can only accept and go out in love towards THE SINLESS. Only two men are sinless--Christ and Mary. Somehow in them, and only in, through and with THEM is anyone SAVED. Holy Mary, pray for us--so that we may be SAVED-SINNERS!

In Pauline imagery, THESE TWO, "are the reason for," and "make possible" the totality of the ELECT. The ELECT are such because of Jesus and Mary. The Elect (including Our Lady) are such because of THE MASS--THE EFFECTIVE SAVING MYSTERY. The Mass, as it were, came into being PRIMARILY from God's love of THE ONLY SINLESS

HUMAN PERSON, Mary, and then of God's ELECT (saved-sinners), her children.

Remember that somehow--as Simeon confirmed--Our Lady is HOSTIAM IMMACULATAM. Certainly, if (as is true) Padre Pio was given the UNSEEN stigmata (in his early years) HOW MUCH MORE DID OUR LADY SUFFER FOR OUR SINS? INDEED, AS NO ONE ELSE EVER DID OR WILL DO, OUR LADY PRAYED THE HOLY MASS--in all she did and in all that was "done to her."

Console her Immaculate Heart. Make reparation to her for the myriad of sins committed within and outside of Christ's One and Only Church. Make reparation for YOUR sins. Make reparation for the sins of others.

WHEN--not "if"--<u>THE</u> Canonized Liturgy is restored, the Living Faith of THE Fathers--THE Catholic Faith will be restored. THEN, once again, St. Ephraim's "priest-centeredness," "priest-appreciation" and a "priest-blessed" church and world will flourish:

"O EXTRAORDINARY MARVEL,
O UNSPEAKABLE POWER,
O AWE-INSPIRING MYSTERY OF THE PRIESTHOOD!
O spiritual, sacred, august, and blameless
office that Christ after His coming left to us unworthy ones!
I cast myself down and beg with tears and sighs
that we may consider what a treasure the priesthood is...

THROUGH THE PRIESTHOOD the world acquires salvation, creation receives light; through it the mountains and hills and valleys and caves are filled with a blessed generation, namely that of the monks...

Through it lawlessness has been banished from the world, and discipline now reigns on earth. Through it the devil has been overthrown, and his power destroyed, the dissolute have become leaders toward justice and the ruthless have become decent."

St. Ephraim--One of the Fathers of the Church
THE HYMN OF PRAISE
St. Ephraim died in 374

SÚPPLICES te rogámus, omnípotens Deus: jube hæc perférri per manus sancti Angeli tui in sublíme altáre tuum, in conspéctu divínæ majestátis tuæ: ut quotquot, ex hac altáris participatióne sacrosánctum Fílii tui, Cor✝pus, et Sán✝guinem sumpsérimus, omni benedictióne cælésti et grátia repleámur. Per eúmdem Christum Dóminum nostrum. Amen.

We ask it of Thee, almighty God, bid these offerings be carried by the hands of Thy holy Angel to Thy altar on high, in the presence of Thy Divine Majesty that those of us, who by participating at the altar shall receive the most holy Body and Blood of Thy Son, may be filled with heavenly benediction and grace.

In sublime altare tuam...to the altar on high.

We humbly beseech Thee, almighty God, to command that these our offerings be carried by the hands of Thy holy Angel to Thine Altar on high, in the sight of Thy divine Majesty, so that those of us who shall receive the most sacred Body ✠ and Blood ✠ of Thy Son by partaking thereof from this Altar may be filled with every grace and heavenly blessing: Through the same Christ our Lord. Amen.

We now associate ourselves in the worship offered to the Divine Majesty in Heaven, "on the golden altar," of which the Apocalypse speaks, which is before the throne of God, and which is enveloped in the prayers of the Saints like the smoke of incense and odours, whilst myriads of angels proclaim with a loud voice: "Glory and benediction to the Lamb that was slain" (Apoc viii, 3-4; v, 8, 11-12).

MEMÉNTO étiam, Dómine, famulórum famularúmque tuárum N. . . et N. . . qui nos præcessérunt cum signo fídei, et dórmiunt in somno pacis. Ipsis, Dómine, et ómnibus in Christo quiescéntibus, locum refrigérii, lucis et pacis, ut indúlgeas, deprecámur. Per eúmdem Christum Dóminum nostrum. Amen.

One of the four purposes for THE Mass is to effect one's love for others--especially for the lessening of Purgatorial pains. Let us remember our loved ones and those who have no one else to pray for them. Here is an act of great fraternal charity.

The Sacrifice of Mass is offered for all of those who somehow rest in Christ--those in the awful purifying fires of Purgatory. From the very beginning of Catholicism, priest-Masses were offered for the deceased.

Be mindful, also O Lord, of Thy servants and handmaids N. . . and N. . . who are gone before us with the sign of faith and who sleep the sleep of peace. To these, O Lord, and to all who rest in Christ, grant, we beseech Thee, a place of refreshment, light and peace. Through the same Christ our Lord. Amen.

Purgatory is "most real." If you love anyone you will pray for their salvation from Hell and the mercy of God toward them in the most awful purifying fires of Purgatory.

THE PRAYER FOR THE PRIEST

FOR ETERNAL HAPPINESS

NOBIS quoque peccatóribus fámulis tuis, de multitúdine miseratiónum tuarum sperántibus, partem áliquam, et societátem donáre dignéris, cum tuis sanctis Apóstolis et Martyribus: cum Joánne, Stéphano, Matthía, Bárnaba, Ignátio, Alexándro, Marcellíno, Petro, Felicitáte, Perpétua, Agatha, Lúcia, Agnéte, Cæcília, Anastásia, et ómnibus Sanctis tuis: intra quorum nos consórtium, non æstimátor mériti, sed véniæ, quæsumus, largítor admítte. Per Christum Dóminum nostrum.

Striking his breast, THE PRIEST interrupts the silence of the Canon and says these three words: nobis quoque peccatoribus. THE PRIEST asks God not to forget or overlook "the priests themselves who offer" (Summa theol. IIIa, q. 83, a.4) this Eucharistic Sacrifice.

Holy Mary pray for us SINNERS. How very very few can profitably confess Reality--"I am a SINNER." I covet above all else God's Mercy in and through Christ's Sacrifice.

THE PRAYER FOR THE PRIEST

FOR ETERNAL HAPPINESS

To us also thy sinful servants, who put our trust in the multitude of Thy mercies, vouchsafe to grant some part and fellowship with Thy holy Apostles and Martyrs: with John, Stephen, Matthias, Barnabas, Ignatius, Alexander, Marcellinus, Peter, Felicitas, Perpetua, Agatha, Lucy, Agnes, Cecilia, Anastasia, and all Thy Saints. Into their company we beseech Thee admit us, not considering our merits, but freely pardoning our offenses. Through Christ our Lord.

How much do you profitably acknowledge that YOU are a sinner, by birth, by inclination, in deed and in habit? ONLY the elect are blessed to see and acknowledge their being sinners unto their salvation through the Mass.

If you profitably confess your "sinfulness" then make this initial sign of your election "ever more sure" by your conforming to Christ Crucified through the graces obtained at Mass.

PER quem hæc ómnia, Dómine, semper bona creas, sanctí✝ficas, viví✝ficas, bene✝dícis, et præstas nobis.

Per ip✝sum, et cum ip✝so, et in ip✝so, est tibi Deo patri ✝ omnipoténti, in unitáte Spíritus ✝ Sancti, omnis honor, et glória.

P. Per ómnia sæcula sæculórum.   S. Amen.

By Christ Jesus (per quem) "these good things" are bestowed on us who comprise THE ELECT. "These good things" are the Eucharistic gifts, the Body and Blood of our Lord, Jesus Christ. By the power of Christ these Eucharistic good things were brought to us in the act of the Consecration.

By this same Lord the sacrificial gifts are "sanctified," "vivified" and "blessed." Through the Sacrifice of the Mass-- through Him, with Him and in Him--all glory and honor are given to God. Here at Mass is fulfilled all of our obligations to God: to adore God; to repar our sins; to thank God; and to love others.

Indeed, it is ONLY through the Saving Deed and the Saving Presence that any thing can and actually does live and is blessed and sanctified unto YOUR good. ONLY Christ and His Sacrifice can redeem or transform Reality unto your good. Otherwise, Reality will curse you NOW and for all eternity.

By whom, O Lord, Thou dost always create, sanctify ✝, quicken ✝, bless ✝, and bestow upon us all these good things.

Through Him, ✝ and with Him, ✝ and in Him, ✝ is unto Thee, God the Father ✝ Almighty, in the unity of the Holy ✝ Ghost, all honor and glory.

P. World without end.   S. Amen.

Through Jesus Christ, the Heavenly Father does always create, sanctify, quicken, bless and procure for us all that is for our good. Only through Christ do "things work out for our good and not for our damnation." Only through Christ are THE ELECT blessed.

Per ipsum. Jesus is our only Mediator. "No one cometh to the Father, but by me" (John xiv, 6). Through Him, forgiveness is granted to sinful humanity. Through Him we are able to satisfy Him Whom we have offended. Through Him, God looks with benevolence upon us; through Him, we can lift up our eyes with confidence towards God. Through Him, God sends His grace to us; through Him, our prayer is heard and our scanty merits are received. Through Him, God comes down to us; through Him we are raised to God. This exchange between Heaven and earth, this coming and going of God to us and us to God is effected on the altar through Him, the Host of our Mass. All the prayers of the Church and all our prayers through the day, that we imagine we make in private and alone, are necessarily joined to the only prayer which reaches Heaven: that of Jesus. His Sacrifice permeates the whole of true religion.

Cum ipso. His Sacrifice transfigures our whole lives. "Without me, ye can do nothing," He said, but with Him, our lives will glorify God on the earth. On the altar, Jesus united us to His perfect obedience, He wants us and makes us victims with Him, victims of duty and for sin, His companions in expiation and the Apostolate.

"In holding the chalice," said St. Francis Borgia, "I have demanded the chalice." "Pray," wrote Msgr. d'Hulst to his sister, "that your brother never be priest without being victim."

We dream of a life of virtue and we bewail our so many fruitless endeavours. Let us try again, but with Him! There is no more powerful means of sanctification than our Mass; the Mass where Christ, "obedient unto death, even the death of the Cross," makes us obedient with Him.

In ipso. Holy Communion perfects the miracle. "He who eateth my flesh," Jesus has said, "abideth in Me and I in him" (John vi, 37). So His life flows out into ours. It assuages our earthly thirst. It dresses our wounds. In Him, we have one mind and one heart. In Him, we give to God the best of our love. In Him, we have good will towards our brethren and devote ourselves to their service; through which we render to God the highest honour and most pure glory. Amen! It is true! Nothing can take the place of our Mass.

In the midst of the old pagan world and under the persecutions of the Emperors, it was at the altar of Holy Sacrifice that Christians drew strength for holy living and courage for martyrdom. They could not miss their Mass, the Dominicum, as they called it.

These three great Christological prepositions also remind us of THE Salutary Dogma. Each human person, except for Our Lady, from conception is NATURALLY destined for Hell, at least as "Limbo-Hell."

1) To get into Heaven one must be baptized in water and the Holy Ghost. One must enter PER CHRISTUM. There is no other way--so Christ told us.

2) Each must then live, as best he can, in communion with Christ's One and Only Church. He must be or live "IN IPSO" or in Christ.

3) Each of us who dies after reaching the age of accountability MUST as it were, die "CUM IPSO"--with Christ or in the state of Sanctifying Grace. Otherwise such will go to "Hell-hell."

NOTE--The Mass-prayers which follow the "lesser elevation," can easily be prayed in the spirit of what has already been noted; OR they are self-explanatory.

Therefore, my comments on these prayers will lessen. However, I urge you to focus on the prayers of the next chapter--those which concern thanksgiving for and appreciation of Holy Communion.

Orémus. Præcéptis salutáribus móniti, et divína institutióne formáti, audémus dícere:

PATER noster, qui es in cælis: Sanctificétur nomen tuum: Advéniat regnum tuum: Fiat volúntas tua, sicut in cælo, et in terra. Panem nostrum quotidiánum da nobis hódie: Et dimítte nobis débita nostra, sicut et nos dimittimus debitóribus nostris. Et ne nos indúcas in tentatiónem.

S. Sed líbera nos a malo.   P. Amen.

LÍBERA nos, quæsumus, Dómine, ab ómnibus malis, prætéritis, præséntibus, et futúris: et intercedénte beáta, et gloriósa semper Vírgine Dei Genitríce María, cum beátis Apóstolis tuis Petro et Paulo, atque Andréa, et ómnibus Sanctis, ✟ da propítius pacem in diébus nostris: ut ope· misericórdiæ tuæ adjúti, et a peccáto simus semper líberi, et ab omni peturbatióne secúri.

The Our Father is prayed since at Mass God's Will is done on earth as He wills it to be done. The Mass is "our power" to bring about God's kingdom by properly loving and forgiving others.

EVILS--PAST, PRESENT AND FUTURE

What is evil? That which is REALLY detrimental to YOU.

What are PAST evils? Unrepented, unconfessed and insufficiently "self-penanced" SINS.

SIN is the ONLY PRESENT EVIL. Why? ONLY sin can put you INTO ETERNAL HELL.

Make this PRIEST'S PRAYER, your prayer. In spirit, join THE PRIEST's prayer.

THE LORD'S PRAYER

Let us pray. Admonished by Thy saving precepts and following Thy divine instruction, we make bold to say:

Our Father, Who art in heaven, hallowed be Thy Name; Thy kingdom come; Thy will be done on earth as it is in heaven. Give us this day our daily bread; and forgive us our trespasses, as we forgive those who trespass against us. And lead us not into temptation.

S. But deliver us from evil.   P. Amen.

Deliver us, we beseech Thee, O Lord, from all evils, past, present and to come, and by the intercession of the Blessed and glorious ever Virgin Mary, Mother of God, together with Thy blessed apostles Peter and Paul, and Andrew, and all the Saints, ✟ mercifully grant peace in our days, that through the bounteous help of Thy mercy we may be always free from sin, and safe from all disquiet.

Pray to God that by your proper prayers, mortifications and "restitutions" God's purifying and purgatorial punishments for YOUR past evils--your PAST insufficiently dealt with SINS--may be LESSENED. Also, pray for God's freely given forgiveness of these sins--that none of them may put YOU into HELL eternally. Similarly pray and resolve regarding PRESENT and FUTURE SINS.

Pray the Holy Mass. Pray that the SALUTARY GRACES of this Mass may apply to you: to lead you to repent and/or properly confess your past sins; to do penance for them; to be graced in the present--this day or this week or until the next Mass you attend--to be freed from or to avoid "present" and future SINS; and, finally that YOUR future in eternity may be FREE FROM THE ONLY ETERNALLY REAL EVIL--Hell.

Free us, O Lord, from all evils--past, present and to come. "Libera nos a malo."

"THE ALTAR is surrounded with angels
adoring the REAL PRESENCE of JESUS CHRIST,
adding their praise and worship with ours."

St. Leonard of Port Maurice
HIDDEN TREASURE
TAN PUBLISHERS

BREAKING OF THE HOST

He uncovers the chalice, genuflects, takes the Host and breaks it in the middle, over the Chalice, saying,

PER eúmdem Dóminum nostrum Jesus Christum Fílium tuum,

He breaks off a Particle from the divided Host,

Qui tecum vivit et regnat in unitáte Spíritus Sancti Deus,

P. Pér ómnia sæcula sæculórum. S. Amen

He makes the Sign of the Cross with the Particle over the chalice, saying,

P. Pax ☩ Dómini sit ☩ semper vobís☩cum.
R. Et cum spíritu tuo.

MIXTURE OF THE BODY AND BLOOD

He puts the Particle into the chalice, saying in a low voice,

HÆC commixtio et consecrátio Córporis et Sánguinis Dómini nostri Jesu Christi, fiat accipiéntibus nobis in vitam ætérnam. Amen.

AGNUS DEI

AGNUS Dei, qui tollis peccáta mundi: miserére
nobis.

AGNUS Dei, qui tollis peccáta mundi:

miserére
nobis.

AGNUS Dei, qui tollis peccáta mundi: dona nobis pacem.

BREAKING OF THE HOST

He uncovers the chalice, genuflects, takes the Host and breaks it in the middle, over the Chalice, saying,

Through the same Jesus Christ, Thy Son our Lord,

He breaks off a Particle from the divided Host,

Who is God living and reigning with Thee in the unity of the Holy Ghost,
P. World without end. S. Amen

He makes the Sign of the Cross with the Particle over the chalice, saying,

P. May the peace ✛ of the Lord be ✛ always with ✛ you.
S. And with thy spirit.

MIXTURE OF THE BODY AND BLOOD

He puts the Particle into the chalice, saying in a low voice,

May this mingling and hallowing of the Body and Blood of our Lord Jesus Christ be for us who receive it a source of eternal life. Amen.

THE LAMB OF GOD

Lamb of God, Who takest away the sins of the world, have mercy on us.

Lamb of God, Who takest away the sins of the world, have mercy on us.

Lamb of God, Who takest away the sins of the world, grant us peace.

Christ's Sacrifice takes away our sins. Christ is our Saviour. For this, we are most thankful.

THE BLESSED VIRGIN RECEIVES HOLY COMMUNION
FROM ST. JOHN

Painting as reproduced
°1994 Vera F. Muller • Metairie LA

COMMUNION

"How happy Jesus makes me!

How sweet is His Spirit!

I am confused.
I do nothing but weep.

What distresses me is that I repay
all this love from Jesus
with so much ingratitude..."

Padre Pio

PREPARATORY PRAYERS FOR THE PRIEST'S COMMUNION

with his eyes directed toward the Sacrament, bowing, he says silently,

PRAYER FOR PEACE AND FIDELITY

DÓMINE Jesu Christe, qui dixísti Apóstolis tuis: Pacem relínquo vobis, pacem meam do vobis; ne respícias peccáta mea, sed fidem Ecclésiæ tuæ eámque secúndum voluntátem tuam pacificáre et coadunáre dignéris: Qui vivis et regnas Deus per ómnia sæcula sæculórum. Amen.

PRAYER FOR HOLINESS

DÓMINE Jesu Christe, Fili Dei vivi, qui ex voluntáte Patris, cooperánte Spíritu Sancto, per mortem tuam mundum vivificásti: líbera me per hoc sacrosánctum Corpus et Sánguinem tuum ab ómnibus iniquitátibus meis, et univérsis malis: et fac me tuis semper inhærére mandátis, et a te numquam separári permíttas: Qui cum eódem Deo Patre, et Spíritu Sancto vivis et regnas Deus in sæcula sæculórum. Amen.

PRAYER FOR GRACE

PERCÉPTIO Córporis tui, Dómine Jesu Christe, quod ego indígnus súmere præsúmo, non mihi provéniat in judícium et condemnatiónem: sed pro tua pietáte prosit mihi ad tutaméntum mentis et córporis, et ad medélam percipiéndam: Qui vivis et regnas cum Deo Patre in unitáte Spíritus Sancti Deus, per ómnia sæcula sæculórum. Amen.

COMMUNION OF THE PRIEST

He genuflects and then says,

PANEM cæléstem accípiam, et nomen Dómini invocábo.

PREPARATORY PRAYERS FOR THE PRIEST'S COMMUNION

with his eyes directed toward the Sacrament, bowing, he says silently,

PRAYER FOR PEACE AND FIDELITY

O Lord, Jesus Christ, Who didst say to Thine Apostles: Peace I leave you, My peace I give you: look not upon my sins, but upon the faith of Thy Church; and deign to give her that peace and unity which is agreeable to Thy will: God Who livest and reignest world without end. Amen.

PRAYER FOR HOLINESS

O Lord Jesus Christ, Son of the living God, Who, by the will of the Father and the co-operation of the Holy Ghost, hast by Thy death given life to the world: deliver me by this, Thy most sacred Body and Blood, from all my iniquities and from every evil; make me cling always to Thy commandments, and permit me never to be separated from Thee. Who with the same God, the Father and the Holy Ghost, livest and reignest God, world without end. Amen.

PRAYER FOR GRACE

Let not the partaking of Thy Body, O Lord Jesus Christ, which I, though unworthy, presume to receive, turn to my judgment and condemnation; but through Thy mercy may it be unto me a safeguard and a healing remedy both of soul and body. Who livest and reignest with God the Father in the unity of the Holy Ghost, God, world without end. Amen.

COMMUNION OF THE PRIEST

He genuflects and then says,

I will take the Bread of Heaven, and will call upon the name of the Lord.

Striking his breast, and saying the opening words audibly, he says three times,

DÓMINE, non sum dignus, ut intres sub tectum meum: sed tantum dic verbo, et sanábitur ánima mea.

Making the Sign of the Cross with the Host over the paten, the priest says,

CORPUS Dómini nostri Jesu Christi custódiat ánimam mean in vitam ætérnam. Amen.

He then reverently receives both halves of the Host.
He uncovers the chalice, geneflects, collects whatever Fragments may remain on the corporal, and purifies the paten over the chalice, saying,

QUID retríbuam Dómino pro ómnibus quæ retríbuit mihi? Cálicem salutáris accípiam, et nomen Dómini invocábo. Laudans invocábo Dóminum, et ab inimícis meis salvus ero.

He takes the chalice, and making the Sign of the Cross with it, he says,

SANGUIS Dómini nostri Jesu Christi custódiat ánimam meam in vitam ætérnam. Amen.

Then he receives the Precious Blood.

COMMUNION OF THE FAITHFUL

Turning toward the people, the priest says,

Misereátur vestri omnípotens Deus, et dimíssis peccátis vestris, perdúcat vos ad vitam ætérnam. S. Amen.

Indulgéntiam, ✝ absolutiónem, et remissiónem peccatórum vestrórum tríbuat vobis omnípotens, et miséricors Dóminus. S. Amen.

The priest elevates a Particle of the Host, turns toward the people, and says,

ECCE Agnus Dei, ecce qui tollit peccáta mundi.

DÓMINE, non sum dignus, ut intres sub tectum meum: sed tantum dic verbo, et sanábitur ánima mea. *(Said three times.)*

He goes to the Altar rail and gives Holy Communion saying to each person,

CORPUS Dómini nostri Jesu Christi custódiat ánimam tuam in vitam ætérnam. Amen.

When all have received he returns to the Altar and replaces the ciborium in the tabernacle.

Striking his breast, and saying the opening words audibly, he says three times,

LORD, I am not worthy that Thou shouldst enter under my roof; but only say the word, and my soul shall be healed.

Making the Sign of the Cross with the Host over the paten, the priest says,

May the Body of Our Lord Jesus Christ preserve my soul unto life everlasting. Amen.

He then reverently receives both halves of the Host.
He uncovers the chalice, geneflects, collects whatever Fragments may remain on the corporal, and purifies the paten over the chalice, saying,

What return shall I make to the Lord for all the things that He hath given unto me? I will take the chalice of salvation, and call upon the Name of the Lord. I will call upon the Lord and give praise: and shall be saved from mine enemies..

He takes the chalice, and making the Sign of the Cross with it, he says,

May the Blood of Our Lord Jesus Christ preserve my soul unto life everlasting. Amen.

Then he receives the Precious Blood.

COMMUNION OF THE FAITHFUL

Turning toward the people, the priest says,

May Almighty God have mercy on you, forgive you your sins, and bring you to life everlasting. S. Amen.

May the Almighty and Merciful Lord grant you pardon, ✝ absolution, and remission of your sins. S. Amen.

The priest elevates a Particle of the Host, turns toward the people, and says,

Behold the Lamb of God, behold Him Who taketh away the sins of the world.

Lord, I am not worthy that Thou shouldst enter under my roof; but only say the word, and my soul shall be healed. *(Said three times)*

He goes to the Altar rail and gives Holy Communion saying to each person,

May the Body of Our Lord Jesus Christ preserve your soul unto life everlasting. Amen.

NOTE: The subsequent chapter on Communion Prayers (Chapter Eight) should prove to be most helpful in "making your Thanksgiving."

THANKSGIVING

PRAYERS AFTER COMMUNION

ABLUTIONS

Wine is poured into the chalice; the priest drinks it and says,

QUOD ore súmpsimus, Dómine, pura mente capiámus: et de múnere temporáli fiat nobis remédium sempitérnum.

Wine and water are poured into the chalice over the fingers of the priest, who dries them with the purificator, saying silently,

CORPUS tuum, Dómine, quod sumpsi, et Sanguis, quem potávi, adhæreat viscéribus meis: et præsta; ut in me non remáneat scélerum mácula, quem pura et sancta refecérunt sacraménta: Qui vivis et regnas in sǽcula sæculórum. Amen.

He drinks the wine and water, and the chalice is purified and veiled.

He goes to the Epistle side and reads the Communion Verse from the Missal.

After THE PRIEST has consumed the Precious Blood, the server pours wine into the chalice while THE PRIEST recites the "Quod ore sumpsimus." Then the fingers of the celebrant are cleansed with wine and water. While this takes place THE PRIEST says the "Corpus tuum Domine."

St. Thomas cautions: "Rinse the mouth after receiving this sacrament lest any particles remain" (Summa theol, IIIa, q. 83, a.5, ad 10). "This is a matter of reverence" (Loc. cit.). Communion in the hand is sacrilege in the hand. As such, it has no place in the Canonized Liturgy.

THANKSGIVING

PRAYERS AFTER COMMUNION

ABLUTIONS

Wine is poured into the chalice; the priest drinks it and says,

Grant, O Lord, that what we have taken with our mouth, we may receive with a pure mind; and that from a temporal gift it may become for us an everlasting remedy.

Wine and water are poured into the chalice over the fingers of the priest, who dries them with the purificator, saying silently,

May Thy Body, O Lord, which I have received and Thy Blood which I have drunk, cleave to my inmost parts, and grant that no stain of sin remain in me; whom these pure and holy Sacraments have refreshed. Who livest and reignest world without end. Amen.

He drinks the wine and water, and the chalice is purified and veiled.

He goes to the Epistle side and reads the Communion Verse from the Missal,

THE PRIEST alone handles Christ. His hands are consecrated. He is consecrated. However, he too must do so reverently.

COMMUNION VERSE

The **COMMUNION VERSE** is a PROPER.
A PROPER changes with each Mass.

At the middle of the Altar he says,

P. Dóminus vobíscum.   S. Et cum spíritu tuo.

*The priest returns to the Missal, saying Orémus,
and begins the Postcommunion.*

POSTCOMMUNION (S)

POSTCOMMUNION PROPER changes
with each Mass.

THE MASS IS NOW ENDED

*Going to the middle of the Altar, he kisses it,
turns to the people and says*

P. Dóminus vobíscum.   S. Et cum spíritu tuo.

P. Ite, Missa est.
S. Deo grátias.

*If it is a day on which the Gloria was omitted, he omits
the Ite, Missa est turns to the Altar and says aloud,*

P. Benedicámus Dómino.   S. Deo grátias.

*In Masses for the Dead, the priest omits the Ite, Missa est,
and without turning to the people says aloud,*

P. Requiéscant in pace.   S. Amen.

The Sacrifice of the Mass has come to an end. "Ite, missa est." And from this, the Mass derives its name--missa; because THE PRIEST sends (mittit) his prayers up to God through the angel, as the people do through THE PRIEST. Or else because Christ is the victim sent (missa) to us; accordingly the deacon on festival days dismisses the people at the end of the Mass, by saying: "Ite, missa est," that is, the victim has been sent (missa est) to God through the angel, so that it may be accepted by God, so states St. Thomas, (Summa theol., IIIa, q. 83, a.4, ad 9).

COMMUNION VERSE

The **COMMUNION VERSE** is a PROPER.
A PROPER changes with each Mass.

At the middle of the Altar he says,

P. The Lord be with you. S. And with thy spirit.
P. Let us pray.

The priest returns to the Missal, saying Orémus,
and begins the Postcommunion.

POSTCOMMUNION (S)

POSTCOMMUNION PROPER changes
with each Mass.

THE MASS IS NOW ENDED

Going to the middle of the Altar, he kisses it,
turns to the people and says

P. The Lord be with you. S. And with thy spirit.

P. Go, the Mass is ended.
S. Thanks be to God.

If the Gloria was omitted the priest omits the Ite,
Missa est, turns to the Altar and says,

P. Let us bless the Lord.
S. Thanks be to God.

In Masses for the Dead, the priest omits the Ite, Missa est,
and facing the Altar says,

P. May they rest in peace.   S. Amen.

"Holy Mass is the offering that is

the most precious,
the most useful,
and the most agreeable

to the Divine Majesty."

St. Peter Julian Eymard

THE LAST GOSPEL

PLÁCEAT tibi, sancta Trínitas, obséquium servitútis meæ: et præsta; ut sacrifícium, quod óculis tuæ majestátis indígnus óbtuli, tibi sit acceptábile, mihíque, et ómnibus, pro quibus illud óbtuli, sit, te miseránte, propitiábile. Per Christum Dóminum nostrum. Amen.

Benedícat vos omnípotens Deus, Pater, et Fílius, ✝ et Spíritus Sanctus.　　S. Amen

P. Dóminus vobíscum.　S. Et cum spíritu tuo.
P. ✝ Inítium sancti Evangélii secúndum
　　Joánnem.　　　　S. Glória tibi, Dómine.

In princípio erat Verbum, et Verbum erat apud Deum, et Deus erat Verbum. Hoc erat in princípio apud Deum. Omnia per ipsum facta sunt: et sine ipso factum est nihil, quod factum est: in ipso vita erat, et vita erat lux hóminum: et lux in ténebris lucet, et ténebræ eam non comprehendérunt. Fuit homo missus a Deo, cui nomen erat Joánnes. Hic venit in testimónium, ut testimónium perhibéret de lúmine, ut omnes créderent per illum. Non erat ille lux, sed ut testimónium perhibéret de lúmine. Erat lux vera, quæ illúminat omnem hóminem veniéntem in hunc mundum. In mundo erat, et mundus per ipsum factus est, et mundus eum non cognóvit. In própria venit, et sui eum non recepérunt. Quotquot autem recepérunt eum, dedit eis potestatem filios Dei fíeri, his, qui credunt in nómine ejus: qui non ex sanguínibus, neque ex voluntáte carnis, neque ex voluntáte viri, sed ex Deo nati sunt. ET VERBUM CARO FACTUM EST, *(here all genuflect)* et habitávit in nobis: et vídimus glóriam ejus, glóriam quasi Unigéniti a Patre, plenum grátiæ veritátis.　　S. Deo grátias.

This gospel passage plus Genesis chapter three are the two Biblical passages that each should memorize. Genesis presents our problem. John presents THE solution. This solution is expressed and lived in each Mass.

May the tribute of my homage be pleasing to Thee, O most holy Trinity. Grant that the Sacrifice which I, unworthy as I am, have offered in the presence of Thy Majesty, may be acceptable to Thee. Through Thy mercy may it bring forgiveness to me and to all for whom I have offered it. Through Christ our Lord. Amen.

May Almighty God bless you, the Father, the Son, ✟ and the Holy Ghost.   S. Amen.

P. The Lord be with you. S. And with thy spirit.
P. ✟The beginning of the holy Gospel according to Saint John. S. Glory be to Thee, O Lord.

In the beginning was the Word, and the Word was with God, and the Word was God. The same was in the beginning with God. All things were made by Him, and without Him was made nothing that was made. In Him was life, and the life was the Light of men: and the Light shineth in darkness, and the darkness did not comprehend it. There was a man sent from God, whose name was John. This man came for a witness, to bear witness of the Light, that all men through Him might believe. He was not the Light, but was to bear witness of the Light. That was the true Light, which enlighteneth every man that cometh into this world. He was in the world, and the world was made by Him, and the world knew Him not. He came unto His own, and His own received Him not. But as many as received Him, to them He gave power to become the sons of God; to them that believe in His name: who are born, not of blood, nor of the will of the flesh, nor of the will of man, but of God. AND THE WORD WAS MADE FLESH, *(here all genuflect)* and dwelt among us, and we saw His glory, the glory as of the Only-begotten of the Father, full of grace and truth.   S. Thanks be to God.

We must note and appreciate that St. John presents the SOLUTION REALISTICALLY--with that particular realism which is an effective ANTIDOTE to the PSYCHOTIC AND SINFUL LOVE AND UNDERSTANDING OF LOVE which prevails in our day. For one thing, God does NOT love UN-conditionally. The ESSENCE of each one's life is to SO LIVE as to be acceptable to the CONDITIONED LOVE of God. (God loves and saves ONLY those who OBEY Him and His Revealed Will.)

The world--MOST of humanity, including alleged Catholics--can't even recognize the Real Christ as their Saviour. They KNOW HIM NOT AS SAVIOUR.

ONLY those who LIVE NOT for or from their own flesh (their bodily desires or natural thinking) and the world (to lust-love or hate people); BUT ONLY, LIVE FOR/FROM GOD'S ENTIRE SALVIFIC WILL-- ONLY THESE WILL BE SAVED FROM ETERNAL HELL.

Do you know and confess yourself to be a great sinner?

ALL of the saints (except Our Lady) did this!

Padre Pio, the Stigmatist-Priest of our century,
was one in spirit with these saints.

When saying his Tridentine or Canonized Holy Mass
Padre Pio's "mea culpa" was accompanied
by deliberate, pronounced and penitent thumps to his chest
indicating to those present that,
conscious of sin,
he confessed himself to be a great sinner.

Usually, the Leonine prescribed prayers (prescribed by Pope Pius XI) are said after Mass. Why? For the conversion of Russia and for our freedom from the temporal and eternal effects of Russia's Errors (the present major Satanic method of attack)--in brief, for our surviving and prospering during this MOST DIFFICULT PERIOD IN THE CHURCH'S ENTIRE HISTORY.

Meditate on these prayers. They are FOR US in this particular age of distress.

By these prayers, the Church ratifies the authentic Fatima Message. RUSSIA AND RUSSIA'S ERRORS are our contemporary enemies.

RUSSIA AND RUSSIA'S ERRORS are "out to destroy us." Until Russia is converted to Catholicism, it REMAINS our enemy and/or God's chosen instrument for our chastisement.

We will attain national and world peace WHEN our enemies--Russia and Russia's Errors--are vanquished by God through the Holy Queen Mary and more specifically, through Russia being consecrated to her AS God commanded at Fatima. We, poor banished children of Eve (naturally), sigh, mourn and weep WHILE we suffer the JUST PUNISHMENTS OF GOD.

We pray to Mary that she may answer our prayer and to bring Jesus to us ETERNALLY--after our brief exile in this most rotten and most horribly cursed world. "Show unto us for all eternity, the Blessed Fruit of thy womb--Jesus." Here in this one prayer, is struck a lethal blow to New Age Catholicism and to all that it represents. Meditate and pray. Here, the essence of life is confronted and resolved.

Then, we pray to God for the CONVERSION of sinners--

fallen away Catholics and non-Catholics (that they may become Catholics). We pray for a FREE AND EXALTED existential church--a church free from its present GROSS CORRUPTIONS and a church even moderately functioning AS God desires. Such a church will be so exalted "that it will convert Russia and most of the whole world. Peace will be given to this world" through such a FREE AND EXALTED CATHOLIC CHURCH.

Finally, we pray to St. Michael--the leader of the angels who battles Satan and his fallen angels in the spiritual realm of THOUGHTS, CLUSTERS OF THOUGHTS and DESIRES. Here is each one's battlefield. We do not merely battle against flesh and blood (cf Eph 6:12). Therefore, we need SPIRITUAL ANGELIC HELP to conquer Satan and his demonic spirit.

Most Sacred Heart of Jesus, have mercy on us. Grant us these salutary requests.

PRAY THE HOLY MASS

"Don't pray at Holy Mass, but pray the Holy Mass...
the highest prayer that exists...

You have to associate your heart
with the holy feelings
which are contained
in THE PRIEST'S words,
and in this manner
you ought to follow
all that happens on the Altar.

When acting in this way
you have prayed the Holy Mass."

His Holiness Pope St. Pius X

PART THREE

PRAYERS AND MEDITATIONS

FOR HOLY COMMUNION

AND FOR THE MASS

"PADRE, DID JESUS DETACH HIS ARMS
FROM THE CROSS TO REST IN YOU?"

"It is I who rest in HIM!"

"HOW MUCH DO YOU LOVE JESUS?"

"The desire is infinite, but in practice, ah me!
I should say zero, and I am ashamed."

Padre Pio
PADRE PIO'S MASS
Fr. Tarcisco of Cervinara

CHAPTER EIGHT

HOLY EUCHARIST PRAYERS

JESUS IS MINE

In Holy Communion Jesus gives Himself to me and becomes mine, all mine, in His Body, Blood, Soul and Divinity. Thus one day, St. Gemma Galgani said candidly to Jesus, "I am Your master."

With Communion, Jesus enters my heart and remains corporally present in me as long as the species (the appearance) of bread lasts; that is, for about 15 minutes. During this time, the Holy Fathers teach that the angels surround me to continue to adore Jesus and love Him without interruption. "When Jesus is corporally present within us, the angels surround us as a guard of love," wrote St. Bernard.

Perhaps we think too little about the sublimity of every Holy Communion, and yet, St. Pius X said that "if the Angels could envy, they would envy us for Holy Communion." And St. Madeleine Sophie Barat defined Holy Communion as "Paradise on earth."

All the saints have understood that a devout Holy Communion means to be possessed by Him and to possess Him. "He who eats My Flesh and drinks My Blood abides in Me and I in him" (John 6:57). It is not possible to have a union of love more profound and more total: He in me and I in Him; the one in the other. What more could we want?

Use the following prayers and meditations before or after Holy Communion. Use them as remote or proximate Thanksgiving and/or preparation for receiving Holy Communion.

OFFERING AND PRAYER OF ST. IGNATIUS LOYOLA
"SUSCIPE"

An indulgence of 3 years.

Take, O Lord, and receive
My entire liberty,
my memory, my understanding
and my whole will.

All that I am and
all that I possess
Thou has given me:

I surrender it all to Thee
to be disposed of
according to Thy will.

Give me only Thy love and Thy grace;
with these I will be rich enough,
and will desire nothing more.

INDULGENCED PRAYER BEFORE A CRUCIFIX

BEHOLD,

O kind and most sweet, Jesus,
I cast myself upon my knees
in Thy sight,
And with the most fervent desire
of my soul

I pray and beseech Thee
that Thou wouldst
impress upon my heart
lively sentiments of
Faith, Hope and Charity,
with true contrition for my sins
and a firm desire of amendment.

While with deep affection
and grief of soul,
I ponder within myself
and mentally contemplate
Thy five most precious wounds;

having before my eyes
that which David spoke
in prophecy of Thee, O good Jesus:

They have pierced my hands and feet;
they have numbered all my bones.

An indulgence of 10 years. A plenary indulgence
may be gained by all, who having confessed and
received Holy Communion, recite this prayer
before an image of Christ crucified
and also pray for the intentions of the Holy Father.

300 days every time. Seven years after Communion.
Plenary indulgence under the usual conditions
once a month for those who recite it every day.

ANIMA CHRISTI

SOUL OF CHRIST,
sanctify me.

BODY OF CHRIST,
save me.

BLOOD OF CHRIST,
inebriate me.

Water from the side of Christ,
wash me.

Passion of Christ,
strengthen me.

O GOOD JESUS,
hear me.

Within Thy wounds,
hide me.

Never permit me
to be separated from Thee.

From the malignant enemy,
defend me.

At the hour of death,
call me.

And bid me come to Thee

That with Thy saints
I may praise Thee
Forever and ever. Amen.

PRAYER OF ST. THOMAS AQUINAS

An indulgence of 3 years.

I THANK THEE, O HOLY LORD, ALMIGHTY FATHER,
ETERNAL GOD,
Who has deigned,
not through any merits of mine,
but out of the condescension of Thy GOODNESS,
to satisfy me, a sinner,
Thy unworthy servant,
with the precious BODY and BLOOD of Thy Son
our LORD JESUS CHRIST.

I pray that this Holy Communion be not
a condemnation to punishment for me,
but a saving plea to forgiveness.

May it be unto me the armor of faith
and the shield of a good will.

May it be the emptying out of my vices
and the extinction of all lustful desires;

an increase of charity and patience,
of humility and obedience, and of all virtues;
a strong defense against all my enemies,
visible and invisible;

the perfect quieting of all my evil impulses
of flesh and spirit, binding me firmly to Thee
the ONE TRUE GOD;

and a happy ending of my life.

I pray too that Thou will deign to bring me a sinner
to that ineffable banquet,
where Thou with Thy Son and the Holy Ghost,

are to Thy saints true light,
fulfillment of desires, eternal joy,
unalloyed gladness, and perfect bliss.
Through the same Christ our Lord. Amen.

ACT OF REPARATION TO THE MOST BLESSED SACRAMENT

With that most profound respect
which divine Faith inspires,
O my GOD and SAVIOUR JESUS CHRIST,
true God and true man,
I adore Thee,
and with my whole heart I love Thee,
hidden in the most august Sacrament of the Altar,
in reparation for all
the irreverences, profanations and sacrileges,
that I, to my shame,
may have until now committed,
as also for all those
that have been committed against Thee,
or that may be ever committed
for the time to come.

I offer to Thee, therefore, O my GOD,
my humble adoration, not indeed,
such as Thou art worthy of,
nor such as I owe Thee,
but such, at least,
as I am capable of offering;
and I wish that I could love Thee
with the most perfect love of which
rational creatures are capable.

In the meantime, I desire to adore Thee
now and always,
not only for those Catholics
who do not adore or love Thee,
but also to supply the defect,
and for the conversion of all heretics,
schismatics, libertines, atheists, blasphemers,
sorcerers, Mahomedans, Jews and idolators.

Ah! yes, my JESUS,
mayest Thou be known, adored and loved by all
and my thanks be continually given to Thee
in the Most Holy and August Sacrament.
Amen.

Indulgence of 500 days each time.
Plenary once a month on the usual conditions,
if recited daily.

THE EUCHARISTIC PRAYERS FROM FATIMA

MY GOD;

I believe, I adore, I hope in and I love Thee.
I ask pardon for those who do not
believe, nor adore, nor hope in, nor love Thee.

MOST HOLY TRINITY,
FATHER, SON AND HOLY GHOST,
I adore Thee profoundly.

I offer Thee the Most Precious
Body, Blood, Soul and Divinity
of Thy Most Beloved Son, JESUS CHRIST,
present in all the tabernacles
throughout the world,
in reparation for all the
outrages, sacrileges and indifferences
by which He Himself is offended.

And through the infinite merits
of His Most Sacred Heart and
the Immaculate Heart of Mary,
I pray for the conversion of poor sinners.

"When THE PRIEST celebrates HOLY MASS,
he honors God,

he rejoices the angels,
he edifies the Church,

he helps the living,
he obtains repose for the dead."

M. Olier

I ADORE THEE, O JESUS

I adore Thee, O Jesus,
true God and true man,
here present in the Holy Eucharist,
humbly kneeling before Thee
and united in spirit with
all the faithful on Earth and
all the blessed in Heaven.

In deepest gratitude
for so great a blessing,
I love Thee, my Jesus,
with my whole heart
for Thou art all perfect
and all worthy of love.

Give me grace
never to offend Thee again
in any way, and
grant that being refreshed
by Thy Eucharistic Presence
here on Earth,
I may be found worthy
to come with Mary,

to the enjoyment of Thy
eternal and beatific
Presence in Heaven. Amen.

The HOLY MASS calls down all spiritual graces:

all the goods appertaining to the soul--
repentance for sins, victory over temptations

whether from external trials such as
bad companions and infernal spirits,
or internal...those arising from rebellious appetites.

The HOLY MASS calls down the aid of grace,
so necessary for enabling us to rise up,
to stand upon our feet,
to walk forward in the ways of God.

It calls down many good and holy inspirations
and many internal impulses, which dispose us
to shake off tepidity

and spurs us on to work our best
with greater fervor, with will more prompt,
with intention more upright and pure;

and these bring with them an inestimable treasure,
being the most effectual means for obtaining from God
the grace of final perseverance,
on which depends our eternal salvation.

St. Leonard of Port Maurice
TAN PUBLISHERS

I FIRMLY BELIEVE

MY GOD, I firmly believe
that Thou art bodily present
in the Blessed Sacrament of the altar.

I adore Thee, here present
from the depths of my heart,
and I worship Thy presence
with all possible humility.

What joy for my soul
to have Jesus Christ
always present with us,
and to be able to speak to Him,
heart to heart
with all confidence.

O Lord, grant that after having adored
Thy Divine Majesty here on earth
in this wonderful sacrament,
I may be able to adore You eternally
in Heaven. Amen.

PRAYER FOR THE RETURN OF THE ROMAN RITE MASS AND LITURGY

O GOD, WHO didst choose Blessed Pius
as supreme Pontiff

in order to shatter the enemies of Thy Church
and to restore the purity of the Sacred Liturgy,

grant us his protection, so that,
cleaving to Thy service
we may overcome the snares
of all our enemies
and enjoy perpetual peace.

Through Christ Our Lord.
Amen.

From the Mass of St. Pius V
May 5

ST. PIUS V, PRAY FOR US!

MAY THAT LITURGY WHICH
YOU MOST DOGMATICALLY DECREED

AS BEING THE CHURCH'S CANON
ONCE AGAIN BE THE CHURCH'S CANON!

CHAPTER NINE

THE "OUR FATHER" AND THE "HAIL MARY"
PREPARE US FOR THE MASS-PRAYER

Pray the Holy Mass by praying the "Our Father" and the "Hail Mary." Since the Holy Mass is the focal point--source, sustainer and perpetual summit--of authentic spiritual life, the Holy Mass must be related to the two most used Catholic prayers.

Strive to say these prayers DIFFERENTLY after--again and again--reading and meditating on this chapter. These Catholic prayers are intimately united to the Holy Mass. As you properly pray them, you likewise properly pray the Holy Mass.

A. Pray the "Our Father"
Pray the Holy Mass

The "Our Father" is most intimately bound up with the Holy Mass. Meditate on the following FACTS.

1) "OUR FATHER"--we live in an "anti-Father age." Why? We live in the end-times (at least the beginning of such times). The end-times' prophet, Elijah, will come to turn the hearts of fathers to their children and the hearts of children to their fathers (Mal 4:5;6). Our times cry out for Elijah. Come Elijah!

Fathers need to be "re-pared"--put back into their GOD-GIVEN roles as chiefs or heads within the Church and within each of their families. The father is head of the wife and of his children--SO WILLS GOD (Eph 5:22; Col 3:18).

Only THE PRIEST, as our spiritual father, celebrates Holy Mass. NOEL's "masses" are celebrated by people--especially women. Look in the sanctuary.

Pray that FATHERS return. Pray that the existential church may be RE-PARED--that it may return to the PAR established by God; and solemnly ratified and clearly practiced by existential churches for over nineteen hundred years. Pray and work for ecclesial REPARATION.

Properly functioning fathers are designed by God: to mirror God the Father; to prepare their wives and children for God as Father; and to lead them to God the Father. So wills God. May His will be done on earth!

God is FATHER. He is THE disciplinarian. He is the ONE Who (through Christ) condemns individuals to eternal Hell; or bestows upon them eternal Heaven--in each case as HE decides. So teaches true Catholicism.

Our father-deprived generation is being deprived of that objective or Father-mirroring DISCIPLINE which each will inevitably confront at his judgment with ETERNAL CONSEQUENCES. Each is NATURALLY Hell-bound. Salvation is God's gift granted to those who are disciplined enough to OBEY HIM and every legitimate and properly functioning representative of Him--or everyone with a "father's role."

The liberal, God-loves-you-as-you-are, mindset of our day ultimately robs us of the ability to relate to God SALUTARILY--seeking the gift of individual salvation from Hell by properly praying and BY LIVING the Holy Mass.

Tolle Patrem, tolle Missam. Take away the proper notion of God the Father and you rob us of even the ability to pray the Holy Mass (unto attaining its purpose).

2) "HOLY BE THY NAME." God the Father is glorified at and by each Holy Mass. Why? His Son glorifies Him by the Unbloody Sacrifice of Calvary.

The Mass is for the glory of God, primarily; and regarding

us, it's for our salvation from Hell.

3) "THY KINGDOM COME." Now is YOUR time of choosing. Do YOU really want God's kingdom to come "FOR YOU?"

Choose to know God and His Will; to love God and to obey HIS will; or, you'll be damned to eternal Hell. In Ignatian fashion, WHICH Kingdom do you choose?

Naturally, you're damned to Hell. Only an adequate (as God judges to be adequate) knowledge, love; and especially, OBEDIENCE to God will save you from the eternal pains of Hell.

Do you really want God's Kingdom FOR YOURSELF? Are YOU willing to obey and will you pay the price of OBEYING GOD THE FATHER and dying to YOUR FLESH and to this world?

4) "GOD THE FATHER'S WILL BE DONE ON EARTH AS IT IS IN HEAVEN." God's will in Heaven is the ETERNAL ADORATION OF THE LAMB WHO WAS ONCE SLAIN (Rev 5:12).

The Holy Mass is prayed for all eternity. For those in Heaven the Holy Mass IS the essence of Heaven. Holy Mass is eternally prayed in Heaven. Therefore, each Holy Mass makes God's Heavenly Will be done on earth AS IT IS DONE IN HEAVEN.

Pray. Meditate. By God's grace, realize this FACT.

What more could you want? What greater event could ever happen "for" you, than a valid or properly-said Canonized Mass of the Roman Catholic Church?

If you are a priest, realize and thank God for His blessings on you. If you are not a priest, become MOST APPRECIATIVE of each validly ordained priest and of each valid priest-celebrated Holy Mass.

Also, console the Two Hearts, since, according to Malachi Martin and others, we have SOME invalidly ordained priests and THUS invalidly consecrated bishops. THESE--few or many--MAKE SACRILEGES of themselves and/or the Holy Mass. Consider also the great number of invalidly said Masses--because of defective form and/or intention. How the present existential church grieves the Two Hearts of Jesus and Mary!

Console the Two Hearts. Make reparation. "At least and at most" offer (as best you can and AS you can) Christ's Sacrifice to God the Father. Pray the Fatima Mass prayer often.

5) "GIVE US OUR DAILY BREAD." Give us the Bread of Life Who comes to each validly said Mass and Who can be received by some at these Masses.

Pray for a greater appreciation of the Holy Eucharist. Thank God the Father for this, THE Daily Bread.

6) "FORGIVE US AS WE FORGIVE OTHERS." God alone forgives SIN, directly and through His validly ordained and validly functioning priests.

At best, we forgive in a similar way. How do we forgive? We GIVE up all hate or lust-love FOR any person.

Don't HATE anyone. Don't lust-love anyone. THEN, you forgive.

Love ONLY and TOTALLY GOD--that's God's first command. Then, relate to (or care for) every creature, including yourself, ONLY AS GOD DESIRES.

If you do this, you will live in the "forgiving mode." You will not need to forgive.

7) "LEAD US NOT INTO TEMPTATIONS THAT WILL BRING US TO SIN."

Instead, help us to grow closer to you, God the Father, through every trial and through every blessing.

8) "DELIVER US FROM EVIL." Your ONLY deliverance is the Mass--the Saving-Deed of Christ.

Pray the Holy Mass. Be delivered from EVIL. Be brought into Heaven.

10) "AMEN"--so may it be AND so will it BE. So may it be for YOU--in your thinking, willing and doing.

AMEN--so may YOU think, will and do unto YOUR salvation from eternal Hell. Ultimately, your choice is to really and fully agree with the "Our Father" or to lose your salvation.

B. PRAY THE HOLY MASS
AS YOU PRAY "THE HAIL MARY"

The main purpose and the Reality of each Holy Mass is TO PRAISE GOD AND TO SAVE THE ELECT. Each Holy Mass both purposes and accomplishes these two goals.

Each Holy Mass glorifies God by saving the Elect. Each Holy Mass is the Sacrifice of Calvary.

At each Holy Mass, pray that you are one of the Elect; and pray that YOU may glorify God in and through the Holy Mass even as you strive to appreciate the Holy Mass as, BEING IN "ITSELF," THE ACT of glorifying God.

Also, throughout the day, let each "Hail Mary" both prepare you for praying the next Mass that you attend or celebrate (if you are a priest) and help you to continue or sustain your previous praying of the Holy Mass.

How then is Mary the Immaculate related to the Holy Mass?

Since each Holy Mass is the EFFECTIVE Saving-Act of Christ, the Saviour, each Holy Mass is the working of the Holy Ghost (in this, the age of the Holy Ghost). By GOD'S WILL, each of the elect is saved through the working of the Holy Ghost; AND, by God's will, the Holy Ghost saves ONLY through Mary, the Immaculata.

Come to more fully realize that the prayer to Mary Immaculate--the Hail Mary--is preparatory to and continues the prayer of the Holy Mass. Why? "Mary, the Immaculata, is THE instrument the Holy Ghost uses in ALL THAT HE DOES IN THE ORDER OF GRACE"--St. Maximilian Kolbe.

This twentieth century saint concludes: "We must be totally Hers! ...All mysteries of grace take place in Mary, full of grace [or THE channel of all graces]." One of the best prayerful ways--outside of attending or celebrating (if you are a priest) Holy Mass--is to believe and to live this and other Catholic dogmas through devoutly saying the "Hail Mary."

PRAY THE HAIL MARY

Let God convince you that the "Hail Mary" has TWO PARTS. At first, you acknowledge and praise God as God and His Will as His Will. Then, YOU pray for yourself as SINNER who needs the Blessed Virgin's prayers in order to avoid your natural fate: eternal Hell.

Now, pray the Hail Mary over and over again until you become convinced of the above truth AND until you are most grateful to God and most happy to pray AS God decrees. Acknowledge and praise God's Will for YOUR salvation; and, petition Mary for her needed help so YOU can avoid eternal HELL.

"Hail Mary, the Lord is with THEE"--God is with Mary; Mary is with God.

As you receive Holy Communion, you receive that Body which Mary gave to Jesus. As you commune with Jesus, you commune with Mary--Jesus is with Her; she is with Jesus.

"Hail Mary THE Channel of ALL graces"--the original Greek states this, not "full of grace." Our Lady is THE one and only channel through which Christ's life, Christ-given graces come to YOU. Why? God so willed it to be.

"Mary is THE Blessed Woman"--blessed is her "fruit," Jesus. She is THE Immaculate Human Person. Christ possessed the Immaculate Human Nature. Mary is the ONLY Immaculate Human Person.

Our Lady is, as St. Maximilian Kolbe pointed out, THE Immaculata--" the material counterpart or manifestation of the Holy Ghost" just as Christ's Human Nature is the same for the Second Person of the Godhead. In a lesser, but like manner Mary IS "unlimitedly" receptive to the infinite love of God in her very person. No other human person is perfectly transparent to divinity. No other human person can be a perfect CHANNEL for God's graces. Only Mary could be the Holy Ghost's Perfect Human Instrument in forming the Church.

Mary is THE MOTHER OF THE CHURCH. This is the age of the Church. This is the age of the Holy Ghost. Mary called forth or called down the Second Person of God's love by God the Father through the Holy Ghost. SHE called down Christ. God loved Mary uniquely and boundlessly.

Christ did NOT come to earth primarily or directly out of LOVE for any or all sinful human people. ONLY Mary called forth Christ the Saviour. Only the IMMACULATA is The Primary and Full Mediatrix--both actively and passively.

She is THE Blessed Mother--the Mother of all who spiritually live; just as, Eve is the mother of all who come to physically live (Gn 3:20). Oh blessed Mother--your Mother and my Mother by the gift of Jesus on the Cross (Jn 19).

The Mother of God was then given to you as YOUR Mother. Jesus Himself wills this to be so. ONLY through Mary can you be united to Jesus.

"PRAY for ME, SINNER"--can YOU pray this prayer? If not, you can't be saved. Christ came ONLY to save adults who acknowledge their sinfulness (those before the age of accountability only need to be baptized by water).

"NOW and at that most crucial time--the hour of final temptations, MY death"--I live in the now. I need help NOW.

However, realize that Satan will unleash ALL of his efforts to turn you from Christ and His Will or to keep you turned from Christ and His Will AT THE FINAL MOMENTS OF YOUR OWN DEATH. Mary is YOUR Mother from Christ's gift (Jn 19).

Pray the Hail Mary. Pray it with great devotion.

Finally, as you pray "now and at the hour of our death," remember NOW is the hour or brief time of your choosing and of your dying. Temporal life is infinitely short compared to the Reality--eternity.

The NOW of your temporal life is of infinite significance. HOW you relate to God--by fully believing in Him or rejecting fully believing the Saving Person; by thankfully and properly praying the Saving-Deed (the Holy Mass); and by sufficiently or insufficiently obeying His Saving Message--determines YOUR eternal MODE OF BEING--in Heaven or in Hell. To avoid Hell, you need HELP--especially, Mary's help.

NATURALLY, you are Hell-bound. Only Jesus can save YOU from Hell. He only does so AS HE DESIRES and He only does so IF you believe, pray and live AS He decrees.

One of God's major decrees is that you can only come to Him through Mary. Pray the "Hail Mary" so you can better pray the Holy Mass.

C. A MYSTICAL "MASS APPLICATION"

The very solemn prayer immediately following the CONSECRATION PRAYERS OF THE CANONIZED LITURGY begins "Unde et memores, Domine, nos servi tui, sed et plebs tua offerimus... hostiam puram, hostiam sanctam..."

"Thence from Heaven (unde) and God's power and from Good Friday being re-done (as much as such can be re-done by God out of its actualization in space and time) or "MEMORES" (as explained elsewhere) one becomes (or MAY become) GOD'S ABJECT SLAVE (nos servi tui) and ONLY THUS one of the people of God (plebs tua)." The above is an amplified and "faith-filled" or "faith-inspired" version of "Unde et memores, Domine, nos servi tui, sed et plebs tua..."

The rest of this PRIEST-PRAYER acknowledges that ONLY those who DE FACTO fulfill the previous description of becoming and being GOD'S PEOPLE, (ONLY THESE) can IN SOME SENSE offer Christ to the Heavenly Father ("...plebs tua offerimus hostiam puram...").

HOW is this most solemn PRIEST-PRAYER reflected in the "Our Father" and the "Hail Mary"?

First of all, the "Our Father" in various places emphasizes "UNDE"--that HEAVEN IS TO COME TO EARTH in similar ways to which HEAVEN--the eternal Effective Salvific Will of Christ as realized on Good Friday--comes to earth at each VALID MASS (also see comments on "Unde et memores" in the chapter directly on Mass Prayers and in Chapter Ten).

As it were, the Mass is to be REALIZED IN AND EXTENDED INTO our daily lives. How? God's Will is to be done by you on earth and THUS will you "hallow" or praise God's Name. ONLY THUS as "servi tui" (God's abject and total SLAVES) can we become "plebs tua" (really one of the People of God).

ONLY THEN does anyone live, not him but Christ in him. ONLY such a one "through, with and in Christ" offers to the Father ("offerimus") HIM ALONE WHO IS ACCEPTABLE AS OFFERING--Christ, the Saviour from SIN.

Secondly, HOW does this most solemn PRIEST-PRAYER (Unde et memores...) find realization, reflection or "roots" in the "Hail Mary"? Let us return to THE PRIEST-PRAYER which immediately preceded "Unde et memores..."

"Blessed are you, Mary, between the TWO WOMEN--between those two who are, according to Scripture's definition 'the MOTHERS OF ALL LIVING.'" EVE is the NATURAL MOTHER of each man. Mary is THE MOTHER of each of the Elect--those few children of Eve who are destined to be "born again."

Because of Adam's sin, Eve naturally "mothers us" unto HELL (the absence of the Beatific Vision with or without eternal hellfires). Because of Christ's Obedience and Saving-Deed, Mary supernaturally "mothers THE ELECT" unto HEAVEN. MARY IS THE BLESSED WOMAN. Eve is the CURSED WOMAN. Eve's children naturally tend to become Satan's OWN for all eternity.

Since Original Sin, each of us (except for the Blessed Mother) is naturally and primarily born of Eve. Each is naturally destined for an eternal void (existence without the Beatific Vision, as explained previously).

"First of nature, then of grace." A few of us will have Mary as our Mother--in time and for all eternity.

This age of the Holy Ghost is the age of MARY. The Holy Ghost came upon Mary to birth Jesus. Mary is the Holy Ghost's PRIMARY "HUMAN INSTRUMENT" similar to the way that Christ's HUMAN NATURE is HIS PRIMARY "HUMAN INSTRUMENT" in defining Him to be Who He is--THE ONE AND ONLY SAVIOUR FROM SIN (the only real and present evil) AND FROM HELL (the only eternal evil); and, positively stated, the "LINK" for each of the Elect (through Mary, His Mother and the Mother of the Elect) TO LIVING FOR ALL ETERNITY THE VERY LIFE OF GOD--IN AS MUCH AS SUCH IS POSSIBLE BY GOD'S POWER FOR EACH PARTICULAR ELECT PERSON.

The Mass is Heaven--in source, sustenance and realization. HOW is Mary the BLESSED WOMAN--the Mother of the Elect--at Mass?

By the Holy Ghost, she is THE Mother. As such, she conceived, birthed and mothered Christ. LIKEWISE, she is THE ONE AND ONLY HUMAN-PERSON-INSTRUMENT OF THE HOLY GHOST in mothering each of the Elect.

By God's Providence and Christ's Salvation, Mary is "THE GIVEN" through Whom each of the Elect must be conceived, born and nurtured. Such is God's Will.

In truth, somehow the PRIEST-CONSECRATION of each Mass extends beyond itself. Somehow, the PRIEST-CONSECRATION is the Holy Ghost making Christ present to mere matter AS He did to "Mary-Matter" in the womb of the Virgin.

HOWEVER, Mary is THE ONLY BLESSED WOMAN. Only through her does the Holy Ghost operate unto salvation in this Age of the Holy Ghost--in this Age of Mary, the Blessed Woman.

So then, somehow in truth, each PRIEST-CONSECRATION PRAYER is a MARY-CONSECRATION PRAYER. As Christ is made present, He comes through Mary, His Mother and THE Holy Ghost's "Instrument."

YET, Christ is ONLY Saviour by SAVING. As it were,

the SAVED or the Elect define Christ to be Christ.

Therefore, each PRIEST-CONSECRATION or each MARY-CONSECRATION births each of the ELECT. Each of the ELECT is born at this GOOD FRIDAY MEMORIAL--the "memores" in the "Unde et memores" of the Mass prayer. The first Mass and its Bloody Realization occurs on the same day--Good Friday, as explained elsewhere.

PRIMARILY, THIS IS CHRIST'S BODY. Secondarily, THIS IS MARY'S BODY AND IN SOME SENSE THIS IS THE BODY OF EACH OF THE BLESSED WOMAN'S OFFSPRING.

Somehow it is true that YOU, IF you are one of the Elect, are conceived and born at each Mass. At each Mass and FROM each MASS YOU, IF you are one of the Elect, are nurtured unto the FULLNESS OF LIFE through your Mother AS Christ WILLS and BY HIS graces and power. Amen.

AMEN--YOU, IN YOUR HERE AND NOW, AT EACH MASS--PRAY THAT SUCH MAY BE FOR YOU. At each Mass, you pray to be Mary's child and because of this God-chosen instrumentality Christ's own. In other words, Christ chooses to save us through HIS OWN WAYS--one of which is the Mass and another of which (from our finite imperfect view, there are other ways) is the BLESSED WOMAN, the Mother of each and every one of the Elect, considering Mary as "God's Given."

"This is MARY'S BLOOD IN YOU which must be shed for sins to be removed." To have Mary as one's spiritual Mother, he must give up his body by shedding his blood.

HOW? Negatively, one MUST DIE to his own flesh (his bodily appetites and dedication to the thinking of his own naturally estranged from God MIND and HEART); and, one MUST DIE to the world (living FOR/FROM other human people in lust-love or hate).

The LIFE that the Holy Ghost gives to the Elect through His created instrument, THE BLESSED WOMAN, IS AND CAN ONLY BE CHRIST'S LIFE.

The Blessed Woman births her own into and with Christ's Life. HOW? As Mother of God and as Mother of the Elect--as sacramentalized and signed by Christ's giving Mary to John at the apex of His Saving-Deed.

With Mary as THE Blessed Woman or THE Mother, each of the Elect will come to live (at least, at the final moments of earthly life) NOT THEM BUT CHRIST IN THEM.

As you pray the Hail Mary, in anticipation and in fulfillment YOU (IF you are one of the Elect) PRAY THE HOLY MASS. The Lord is with Mary. Mary is with the Lord.

She alone is "THE channel of all graces"--thus, THE "Instrument" of the Holy Ghost. Her fruit is Jesus--in Christ, primarily; and secondarily, in each of THE ELECT.

She is THE BLESSED WOMAN--the one and only Mother of all who will live the life of Christ for all eternity (in as much as this is possible for each particular Elect Person).

She is THE Mother of God. That's "our given." She can be YOUR mother. For this, you pray at each Holy Mass AS you PRAY THE HOLY MASS.

YOU, A SINNER, pray for HER PRAYERS--now and in the final moments of your dying. PRAY THE "HAIL MARY." PRAY THE HOLY MASS.

Do you know and confess yourself to be a great sinner?

ALL of the saints (except Our Lady) did this!

Padre Pio, the Stigmatist-Priest of our century,
was one in spirit with these saints.

When saying his Tridentine or Canonized HOLY MASS
Padre Pio's "mea culpa" was accompanied
by deliberate, pronounced and penitent
thumps to his chest
indicating to those present that,
conscious of sin,
he confessed himself to be a great sinner.

CHAPTER TEN

GOOD FRIDAY REPEATED AND
HEAVEN "BEAMED DOWN" TO EARTH

Only THE PRIEST celebrates Mass. As such, he acts or functions "in persona Christi"--in the PERSON of Christ.

That PERSON is the Second Person of the Trinity. God, only God, can effect MASS.

More specifically, ONLY the Second PERSON of the Trinity can effect or celebrate MASS. Pray about this. Thank God for the Mass--His greatest gift to you in your space and time.

In fact, the EXTERNAL GLORY of Heaven is the MASS--the Second Person's ACTUALIZED ACT OF LOVE TOWARDS HIS ELECT through the Blessed Virgin. Here is Heaven--the Second Person's love made present and effective in your space and time.

Each priest in celebrating his valid Mass ACTS in persona Christi, "making present" or renewing in space and time the EFFECTIVE SALVIFIC WILL OF CHRIST AS CHRIST'S UNBLOODY SACRIFICE. Why wasn't any Mass done before Good Friday?

First of all, we should recall that the Jewish day begins at sunset of what we "wrongly" call the previous day--i.e. "Holy Thursday"--and ends at sunset in this case, on Good Friday. Therefore, the First Mass and Its "Realization" happened on THE SAME DAY (according to Jewish reckoning)--Good Friday. Good Friday is THE Day of Salvation--the DAY OF THE MASS.

So each Mass is, as it were, Good Friday coming to us out of eternity into our peculiar space and time and "returning" UNTO eternity. Each Mass IS the EFFECTIVE Saving-Deed of Christ made present in our space and time.

Good Friday (as defined by the God-given Jewish calendar) is THE DAY OF SALVATION--the day of the Mass. After Good Friday only a valid priest who acts NOT "in Christ's name" BUT "in Christ's very Person," can say Mass.

In God's economy, NO ONE was allowed to do so until the priesthood was established by Christ on "Holy Thursday" (which is REALLY Good Friday) and NO ONE can so do except a validly ordained priest.

On Good Friday itself, Christ as it were, DID THE UNBLOODY AND THE BLOODY SACRIFICE. The Bloody Sacrifice is the Prime Sacrifice of the Mass or the "source, sustenance and COMPLETENESS or Realization" of each Mass. We are saved by THIS GOOD FRIDAY SACRIFICE in either of its forms--the Mass or "Calvary Itself."

It is YOUR great privilege to have Good Friday repeated at every valid Mass that you attend. In as much as THIS, THE Sacrifice, can be repeated by Christ, it IS repeated at every VALID Mass by a validly ordained priest as he properly acts "in PERSONA Christi."

What a priceless treasure Christ has handed over to us and to the hierarchy (to preserve, to renew and to properly hand on). In OUR day, console the Sacred Heart and the Immaculate Heart as this treasure at least is being subjected to the possibility of "greatest sacrilege" WITHIN Christ's own Church by his very own and especially by the UPPER hierarchy.

Pray and work to totally remove such MEGA-NEGATIVITY. Pray and work for COMPLETE ECCLESIAL REPARATION.

Thank God for allowing you to attend even ONE valid Mass in your lifetime. Show your gratitude by attending as many valid Masses as you can; and, by supporting and promoting any and all bishops and priests who POSITIVELY live and work so that this priceless treasure may be clearly disclosed so as to be properly reverenced; validly repeated; protected from sacrilege; and properly handed on to posterity.

Remember, each valid Mass brings the essence of Heaven into YOUR space and time. HERE, also, is THE HEAVEN OF THE ELECT redeemed by the Lamb that was once slain. HERE too is Good Friday--Christ's Mass in THE Sacrifice.

HERE the Lamb Who was once slain comes to you as the One Who alone through His Renewed Saving-Action makes Heaven possible for you and actualizes Heaven for each of His Elect.

Adore Christ. Reverence to the utmost EACH VALIDLY ORDAINED PRIEST. Such priests are God's greatest instruments of salvation this side of death. SINCE through them and them alone the Saving-Action, the Saving-Person and effective Salvation Itself comes into our space and time.

UNDE ET MEMORES

So begins the first prayer immediately following the most solemn time of THE PRIEST'S Mass--the Consecration. "Unde et memores" are the first words of this august prayer.

"UNDE"--Heaven which is defined by God in His Apocalypse as the "adoration of the Lamb that was slain (Apoc 5:11-14)" comes thence to us. Christ's ever-continuing (eternal) salvific WILL breaks into our space and time through a valid priest and his valid Mass. "UNDE" becomes Heaven Itself--the ADORABLE AND HEAVEN-DEFINING Unbloody Lamb-Slain.

"MEMORES"--Good Friday, the DAY of the FIRST MASS AND BLOODY SACRIFICE IS MADE PRESENT (as much as God can do so AT EACH VALID MASS). Remember, the Jewish day began at sunset on what we "wrongly" call Holy Thursday and ended on Good Friday--thus Christ's "Holy Thursday" Mass is REALLY His Good Friday Mass.

For a more extensive treatment of this subject read Chapter Ten on the relationship of the Mass to Heaven and Good Friday. Pray the Holy Mass by coming to a better comprehension of this Great Mystery of Faith. Out of this "double mystery"--as "contained in" and referred to by "unde et memores"--comes the GRACED POSSIBILITY of our being or becoming "nos servi tui et plebs tua sancta."

Notice the order. First, we "gracedly" imitate Mary and become as best we can "servi tui"--God's SERVANTS or SLAVES. Only then can we become "plebs tua"-- God's people or the REAL (not merely bragged about in a futile manner) PEOPLE OF GOD.

> "By means of the unbloody immolation
> (in the august sacrifice of the altar)
>
> the HIGH PRIEST (Jesus Christ)
> continues to do that which
> He already did on the Cross
>
> by offering Himself
> to the Eternal Father
>
> as the only
> and most acceptable Victim."
>
> Pope Pius XII
> MEDIATOR DEI
> 1947

CHAPTER ELEVEN

A SPECIAL MEDITATION ON THE FIVE WOUNDS

I.   THE DIVINE FEET OF JESUS--Thy divine, yet human, feet teach me and "grace me" to go and to be WHERE You want me to go and/or to be. Thy divine feet--from Thy conception on--were totally obedient to the Father's will. Thy divine feet won for me the graces to go and to be WHERE You want me to go and to be.

Help me then to perceive and to remove: all selfish ambition, laziness, discontent, anger and the like--which not only sour my consecration to Thee, but which are SINS. Positively, teach me and "grace me" or help me, to be virtuously industrious for the accomplishment of Thy will in my life--especially, concerning the WHERE of my life.

II.   THE FLESH WOUNDS OF JESUS--Thy adorable Body suffered much during Thy lifetime, especially at the Scourging. Thy Body was and is sacramental. Thy Body tells me HOW I am to live even as I am given graces by Thy sufferings to live as I should.

May I always be or may I become convinced that my flesh, my brain and my body, and the world, the natural unredeemed or unsanctified communities of men--ecclesial and social--are my enemies. They can bring me to an eternal Hell. May I be graced to mortify my flesh and to despise the world.

Grace me especially, O Lord Jesus, to see HOW I am living for my flesh and this world. By Thy sufferings and by the "compassionate" suffering of Thy Mother, Mary, grant me the graces not only to perceive my sins; but also, to eradicate them.

Grace me to live CRUCIFIED WITH THEE. Grace me to live crucified to my flesh and to this world.

III. THE DIVINE HANDS OF JESUS--Thy divine, yet human hands teach me and "grace me" to DO what You want during my brief life on earth. From the beginning of Thy human life, Thy adorable hands did God the Father's will--as an example for me and to give me the grace to do as You desire and thus to be saved from Hell and be with Thee for all eternity in Heaven.

Grant me, O Lord Jesus, the grace to be content and industrious in doing Thy will--beginning with the Ten Commandments to doing each of my daily duties as You desire. I need Thy graces to do Thy will. I thank Thee for Thy graces. In a special way, I thank Thee for Thy graces which have allowed me to do Thy will and thus to live freed from: fear, worry, frustrating self-ambition, jealousy, unresolvable regrets and similar "fruits" which come from living for/from this world and/or my flesh.

IV. THE CROWN OF THORNS--Thy skull was pierced with thorns. In this way, You "graced me" and taught me to THINK as You desire. I am to have or to come to have every thought subject to Thee (II Cor. 10:5).

"Grace me" to THINK as You desire--to be aware of my actual thinking and then to confess my sinful THINKING as well as my helplessness in THINKING as I should. Help me to cooperate with Thy graces so as to come to think as You desire. I also thank Thee for Thy graces of the past and Thy present graces which lead me to desire or "to possess" this great blessing.

V THE PIERCED HEART--Thy adorable human Sacred Heart was pierced for me. Thus, Thou "graced me" and taught me to desire only God and God's will.

I now recall the great Fatima Vision at Tuy. In this vision, You taught us many great truths. In this vision, You confirmed the great truth that sin is the only and greatest present evil; and that loving-kindness or grace and mercy come from Thee through Thy Mother, Mary, and through the Holy Sacrifice of the Mass and Holy Communion. In Thy way, You save us from sin and Hell.

Help me to live my consecration. Help me to desire only what You want. Help me to come to Thee through my consecration to Mary.

Help me, dear Jesus, to come to desire as the only perfect human person, Mary, desired. Help me to live consecrated to Mary--desiring to do only God's will. Help me to desire or to love Thee totally and exclusively. Then I will be living my consecration perfectly.

"He who in life is in the habit
of devoutly hearing HOLY MASS
shall in death be consoled

by the presence of the angels
and the saints, his advocates,
who shall bravely defend him
from all the snares of infernal spirits."

Christ Our Lord to St. Mechtilde
1.3, Grat. Spir. c. 27

CHAPTER TWELVE

CORPUS CHRISTI

As THE PRIEST gives Holy Communion, he first makes the Sign of the Cross with the Sacred Host over each individual communicant. He says:

"Corpus Domini Nostri Christi custodiat animam tuam in vitam aeternam, Amen." "May the Body of Our Lord Jesus Christ preserve or keep your soul unto eternal life. Amen."

So does THE PRIEST bestow Christ and Christ's Benediction on each communicant in the Canonized Liturgy. You may wonder HOW Benediction comes in. Benediction is bestowed as THE PRIEST "makes the Sign of the Cross over you with the Blessed Sacrament" as he gives each communicant the Eucharist.

In the Canonized Liturgy, each communicant receives his own personal Benediction. Pray about this. Be thankful.

"May the Body of Our Lord Jesus Christ bring and preserve your soul INTO eternal Heavenly life." Each of us will live forever. Each CAN only live forever in Heaven through Christ or through CORPUS CHRISTI.

ONLY Jesus saves from eternal Hell. Each is born estranged. Each is born FOR HELL--at least, for limbo-Hell. No one can get to Heaven NATURALLY.

So teaches the REAL Catholic Church. So, "deep down," each cognizant human person feels or realizes. People experience this NEED to such an extent that they are compelled to satisfy it--even in a futile manner. Thus, MEN are led to create their own false religions.

ONLY Christ and His One and Only Religion--or continuing Plan and Action for Salvation--can save YOU from Hell. Extra ecclesiam, NULLA est Salus.

NO ONE can be saved outside of the Church. At the very least, one must join the Church by Baptism and then NOT leave it by serious SIN--even one sin of disbelief or one serious sin of the Flesh.

Heretics and flesh-sinners CANNOT BE SAVED. Without full or complete FAITH, one can't be saved (1 Col 4:22; Jn 5). Nothing of the FLESH can enter Heaven (Jn 1:14; Ro 3:20; Ro 8).

HOW are YOU to be saved from YOUR FLESH; YOUR living for/from other people (THE WORLD); and, from your naturally following plans and programs NOT from Christ? By the Blood of the Lamb, by the Body of Christ, by CORPUS CHRISTI.

You have a body and a unique soul. Your soul IS you. Your soul uses or expresses itself through your body. Also, your body, to some extent, determines, influences and defines "you"--your soul.

Notice the Church's Canonized fiducial and liturgical statement at Communion time. "May the BODY of Christ bring your soul into eternal life."

Somehow and somewhat, YOUR soul must link up to CHRIST'S BODY for you to go into Heaven. Think about THIS.

To be saved from Hell, your body (natural bodily appetites and natural thinking and natural desiring) must DIE. As it were, CORPUS CHRISTI must take the place of your natural body (on earth or through the awful and most horrible purifying fires of Purgatory).

Those who can't link up to Christ's BODY MUST go into eternal separation--eternal Hell. Why? Christ's Blood or Christ's Body IS the only Source, Sustenance and Summit of Heaven for the Elect.

"Worthy is the Lamb that was slain and now defines Heaven for the Elect to receive the Elects' praise and thanksgiving for ever and ever"--Rev 5:12. The Body of Christ--CORPUS CHRISTI--is Heaven for the Elect.

Here is the REALIZATION of that metamorphosis or TRANSFORMATION OF ONE'S SOUL that St. Paul demanded of each of Christ's Elect (Rm 12:2). Here is THE WAY for you to eventually become a TOTALLY RE-NEWED or glorified, SOUL (Rm 12:2). Corpus Christi is THE means--both NOW and forever. As it were, CORPUS CHRISTI is the BODY which defines each soul as being Christ's.

Each soul must be purified to enable it to be capable of eternal transformation into Christ. Each soul can only be so transformed by the Blood of the Lamb--by Corpus Christi.

Here we see the sanctity of our bodies. They are being transformed into death. They are being transformed into life. They are to be even now, somehow and somewhat, CORPUS CHRISTI.

Each must die to live. Each must die to his own flesh and to this world. WHY? Nothing of either can or will go into Heaven. Both will be burnt up or somehow be part of Hell (2 Pe 3:10; Re 18:8; Re 21:6). Each must come to "live Christ (Phlp 1:22; Ga 2:20)" or be damned eternally.

Even now--DURING TRANSFORMATION BY YOUR DYING "BY, WITH AND IN" CHRIST, YOUR body is somehow and somewhat Christ's (Phlp 1:22; Ga 2:20). Therefore, St. Paul demands that you treat your body as such (2 Co 6:16).

IF your body is Christ's, your body will demand that it DIE TO LIVE. Why? Christ's earthly body was, as it were, under this compulsion. "IT" lived in FULL obedience to God's Will. "IT lived so dyingly" that "IT had to" suffer extreme agony (Jn 18:37; Phlp 2).

As you live in obedience to God's Will--as you live, not you, but Christ in you--your body will be transformed. Thus are you baptized by the Holy Ghost (Ro 6:3; Ac 1:5).

The Holy Ghost operates in this His Age, which is the Age of Mary. St. Maximillian Kolbe concluded from his mystical insights that the Blessed Virgin is the one and only Primary Agent or Instrument of the Holy Ghost.

The Second Person chose to act IN and through His own unique human nature. The Word of God became Flesh. Jesus Christ came to be for the salvation of His Elect.

Similarly, the Holy Ghost chooses to act through the one and only SINLESS human person, the IMMACULATA. Our Lady is uniquely blessed as the Mother of all who are saved-- the Mother of the Church.

If one can allow God to DO AS HE PLEASES and one accepts His "good pleasure"--then, classical saints assure us, this is a sign of one's election. Specifically, true devotion to Mary is a sure sign of one's election.

The Word was made FLESH in Mary. Corpus Christi is Mary's flesh. Similarly, the Elect are such only by having Mary as their Mother by the Holy Ghost's actions.

As it were, the Holy Ghost continues the action of "making" CORPUS CHRISTI and those who "incorporated into Him" to become the Mystical Body. Now, in the age of the Holy Ghost and of Mary, the Holy Ghost continues INCARNATION. He is building up Mary's Body--the Mystical Body of Christ.

However, now He does this in the souls of His Elect by transforming them by death somehow and eventually through the Body of Christ. Such souls constitute the Church--the Elect--forever and even NOW (in seed and in anticipation).

How eagerly and thankfully does one of the Elect come to

Holy Communion! Unless one eats and "becomes" Christ's Body--he cannot have any true life in Him (Jn 6:51-56).

Corpus Christi must become your body OR you will die eternally in God's eternally burning trash heap of Hell. How does Christ's Body become yours? By "eating" in obedience to His Will or by properly receiving Holy Communion (if, and when you can, of course).

Christ's Body becomes YOURS not by "mechanically" assimilating "IT." St. Paul assures us that some receive Holy Communion unto their GREATER eternal damnation (1 Col 1:21-27).

God is never to be mocked. As one sows, so will he reap (Ga 6:8).

Receive Holy Communion properly and profitably OR be further damned by your blasphemy. In North America today, most communicants receive unto their further condemnation. MOST Catholics disbelieve in one or more Catholic Truths; and many live in the perpetual mega-sin of PRESUMPTION.

The "validly confected" Holy Eucharist is ADORABLE. "IT" is Heaven. Corpus Christi is the one and only LIFE of each of God's ELECT.

As best you can discern, make sure that you are receiving a "validly confected" Sacred Host. Today, in North America, some Masses are invalid--because ordaining bishops weren't themselves validly ordained as priests, because priests weren't validly ordained; or because Masses aren't validly said.

Indeed, it's a "two-way situation." We are deprived of true Sacred Hosts because of our extreme sinfulness.

Salvation and the sacraments ARE God's GIFTS--not, our DUE. NOW, the withdrawal of such GIFTS shows not only a withdrawal of God's mercy; but also, an infliction of God's punishments.

Where God freely and truly gives CORPUS CHRISTI--make sure that you respond as BEST you can to this "open-ended challenge and duty." Be humble. Be thankful.

YOU can never be thankful enough. Our adoration on earth will never be adequate. However, not to ADORE would be sinful.

MAKE the SOURCE AND SIGN OF YOUR ELECTION SURE (2 Pe 1:10). How? By God's graces, seeing, appreciating and properly responding to the great mystery among us--CORPUS CHRISTI.

THE ROSARY is like MARY--it leads you to JESUS.

As your prayerful attention goes to MARY,

it is directed to OUR SAVIOUR and His Saving Deed.

"Grant us, we beseech Thee, O Lord,
to be filled with the eternal enjoyment
of Thy Divinity, which is prefigured
by the reception of Thy precious
Body and Blood in this life."

CHAPTER THIRTEEN

MINI-MEDITATIONS ON THE MASS

There follows a small collection of mini-meditations on the Mass. Use them during your "quiet times." Let them carry through into your days.

You can add to these by focusing on one or two priest-prayers from the Canonized Liturgy. Pray them. Meditate on them. These prayers come from Christ through the Apostolic Tradition of the Church (Christ among us).

You can also add to these mini-meditations, other meditations of your own which you glean from reading this and other books. Perhaps, you will want to mark certain pages for this purpose.

-1-

BEFORE THE NEXT MASS

Look forward to the next Mass. Become properly thankful for Christ's Saving Action coming to YOU in your space and time. What an indescribable privilege--even if you could attend only ONE Mass in your lifetime.

Here at Mass, is Calvary--Calvary re-done as best God can re-do the ONCE AND FOR ALL OF THIS SAVING-EVENT FOR HIS ELECT. For all eternity, THIS SAVING-ACTION will be re-done IN the Saving-Person, Jesus Christ. SUCH is Heaven.

Why and HOW? Christ is defined as Saviour. For all eternity, the Lamb Who was slain is the "object" of all praise, adoration and thanksgiving (Rv 5,8). He, Christ, IS Heaven.

SALVATION--as SAVING PERSON and as Act--is Heaven. THIS is each Mass. Confess your blindness and your coldness FOR not appreciating THE ONLY IMPORTANT REALITY.

-2-

HOLY MARY, HELP ME

Who is the "object" of each Mass? Confessed, repenting and Christ-focused SINNERS. These, who are God's elect, are God's external Mass-glory. Other sinners will be damned to eternal Hell.

Holy Mary, Mother of God, pray for us, ROTTEN SINNERS. Liberal Catholics--"sinless" New Agers--don't like the Real Mass. They refuse to accept the Mass for what "it" is. In fact, their experts invent liturgies to these wicked people's liking.

Are you a VICTIM of the NEW CHURCH? Do you see, confess, repent of; and, turn to Christ because of YOUR SINS? Really? Or, are you a "normal Catholic?" Are you BLIND to your sins?

Can you pray the "Hail Mary?" MOST--nearly all-- American "Catholics" CAN'T. Why? They can't properly admit that they are sinners. Most of them can't even admit that SIN exists and that THEY SIN, as many surveys conclusively prove.

Holy Mary, Mother of God, help me to be your child. I petition you: "PRAY FOR ME, A HORRIBLY ROTTEN SINNER", at the hour of "each Mass."

SOLUS CHRISTUS

Only Christ saves. He saves by His Mass--the unbloody Sacrifice of Calvary.

For sinners, here is their one and only HOPE. Here is the SAVING-ACTION coming across space and time from Calvary to each valid Mass and eternally lighting up all of the elect with Heavenly Bliss.

Only Christ saves. He alone is SAVIOUR for sinners. IF you appreciate CHRIST, you will appreciate HIS SAVING-ACTION through which His Saving-Person comes to us and abides with us "in" the Holy Eucharist.

BE HUMBLE, NOT PROUD

Mea culpa, mea maxima culpa--through my fault and even through my grave fault have I SINNED. Christ is Saviour for SINNERS. The Mass is the Saving-Act for SINNERS.

The total ambience of CL (the Canonized Liturgy) screams forth: At best, YOU are a SINNER. NOEL double-speaks and as it does, it leads the proud to become ever more blinded and fixed in their demonic pride.

Be humble. Appreciate the "humbling prayers" of the Latin Rite's CANONIZED liturgy. Let these prayers color your whole day.

YOU are a SINNER. "Holy Mary, pray for me, a SINNER, now and at the hour of my death."

BE RECONCILED TO YOUR BROTHER

"Go first to be reconciled to your brother, and then come and offer your gift." What is your gift, if you aren't a priest?

Your gift is your conforming to Christ. To conform to Christ, AT LEAST you must not HATE others and you should not have any outstanding "unresolved" FRATERNAL INJUSTICES.

In the Canonized Liturgy, Catholics focus on God, not MEN. However, in order to really worship God, YOU must be in the state of sanctifying grace--a Catholic without mortal sin on his soul.

Therefore, do all you can (by God's grace, of course) to be in that condition BEFORE going to Mass, although going to Mass in serious sin may help you to properly repent. The Mass is only effective for the ELECT. Do all YOU can to be one of the elect.

THE SACRAMENT THROUGH THE SACRIFICE

The Eucharist comes into being ONLY as a result of THE Sacrifice being "re-made" by a properly functioning and valid priest as he acts IN PERSONA CHRISTI. Out of or from the Unbloody Sacrifice of the Mass comes CHRIST: Body, Blood, Soul and DIVINITY under or "to" that which APPEARS to be bread.

During the day, try to come to a better appreciation of THIS ADORED REALITY. Try, by God's grace, to SEE and to properly respond to THE MOST AWESOME AND ADORABLE REALITY.

We are so miserably cursed by SIN--original and actual--
that very few of us have even an inkling of THE MOST
ADORABLE REALITY.

Pray. Meditate. Petition God the Holy Ghost for:
understanding, wisdom, piety and proper FEAR of God.

BE TRANSFORMED

New Agers attend Mass pretending that they will be or
have already been TRANSFIGURED with Christ. NO! The
only way--this side of death--you can be in any way
transformed into Christ is by your painfully dying to YOUR
FLESH AND THE WORLD "in" and "through" Christ.

Here, at Mass, you are given the Suffering Christ--His
Transformation; His Unbloody Sacrifice. Let this mind and
heart be in you by Christ's Mass-graces. The Mass ISN'T a
banquet. The Mass IS Sacrifice--THE Sacrifice for YOUR
SINS.

Resolve to properly "sacrifice." Resolve to suffer and die-
-to die to your natural body and mind; and what they naturally
want; and to die to pleasing others. Resolve to please ONLY
GOD. Resolve to suffer and die with Christ.

To be transformed into Christ, YOU must let Christ LIVE
in you AS He demands. WHENEVER Christ lives in any
mortal body, He leads it to its death--death to its flesh and to
the world (to the desire to please people; or to be praised by
people; or to dominate/hate people).

ASK AND RECEIVE

Our me-generation asks selfishly or wrongly and so, at best, imagines that God answers its prayers. Look at CL's prayers. What do these canonized prayers ask? Salvation, only salvation.

What "kinds of" salvation are prayed for? The full enjoyment of salvation for those in Purgatory. Our own salvation (being brought into Heaven); AND, any and all "things" (suffering, misfortunes, mutilations, opportunities, etc.) that will render this SALVATION ACTUAL ("incolumitatae"--those things which won't impede us in attaining salvation).

That's ALL the Canonized Mass prays for. That's all we pray for. That's ALL you need to pray for.

What would it profit you IF you were granted 100 years of robust health and twenty million dollars a year AND you went to Hell forever? Pray only for salvation. ONLY pray to be saved from Hell eternal. PRAY THE HOLY MASS.

Recognize and renounce the pseudo-religious worldly attitude which prevails today. Embrace the gospel SPIRIT of THE Canonized Liturgy. Pray this liturgy all day long--at least in spirit.

BE HUMBLED TO BE EXALTED

He who humbles himself WILL BE exalted. At least one must be humble enough to accept the Mass as IT is--the Unbloody Sacrifice (not MEAL) of Calvary.

At least one must be humble enough to wholeheartedly accept every one of the Real Church's Official and Binding Dogmas and Teachings--from its condemnation of "contracepting" to its dogmas on the Mass. Be humbled-- submit your mind and heart to truth; to God's Revelations.

FEW alleged Catholics in the U.S.A. are humble enough to be REAL Catholics. MOST American "Catholics" (including clerics) are so evil that they are ipso facto excommunicated for refusing to believe in all of the essential and binding church teachings.

If you are one of the few, make the sign of your election sure BY growing in true humility and resisting subtle temptations to be proud.

-10-

PREPARING FOR THE TEST

YOU have an appointment that you can't break. It is appointed unto YOU to die and to be JUDGED BY GOD according to HIS standards.

We are in such a horribly psychotic and sinfully presumptuous generation that MOST American "Catholics" IN EFFECT deny their Particular Judgment. They can deny death and judgment; BUT death and judgment will inevitably come.

"God's too good to send anyone to Hell...I'll get to Heaven as long as I do what I think is RIGHT...God's merciful to all..."

These and hundreds of other demonic deceptions are blinding MANY and leading them into ETERNAL HELL.

At each Mass, pray that the Mass IS for you--that you are one of the recipients of THE Saving-Action of Christ.

Remember to often renounce the very popular mega-sin of PRESUMPTION. Hope is that God-given mega-virtue which allows one to be convinced that by God's grace and one's graced cooperation that he is able to live as God demands; and thus to attain eternal happiness in Heaven.

-11-

CHRIST--JUDGE AND SAVIOUR

St. Augustine, reflecting Catholic Teaching, assures us that God will judge each JUSTLY. However, His Saving Mercy will not be extended to ALL.

Those who go to Hell forever will JUSTLY go. Those who go to Heaven will be the recipients of God's freely bestowed Saving MERCY. God is in charge, not YOU.

What can YOU do? Make the SIGN (S) of your election sure.

Do all you can--BY GOD'S. GRACES AS OBTAINED BY THE CALVARY-MASS--to "be or become" (from your limited and imperfect view) ONE OF THE ELECT; OR, PART OF THE MASS (which, according to Church Dogma, is the EFFECTIVE Salutary Action).

In effect, ONLY the elect are PART of THE Mass. Properly build on and "perfect" the Signs of your election-- that YOU were baptized, that you have lived and believed as a TRUE Catholic; and have been blessed to attend (or celebrate, if you are a priest) MASS--so that you will be numbered among THE ELECT.

PUT GOD BACK IN THE MASS

Each Catholicism-Canonized Mass is THE Act of praising God. It isn't liturgy as the work of men. Each Mass is the PRAISE OF GOD BY CHRIST, not by mere mortals.

God is praised in Himself and FOR Himself. Also, He is praised as manifested, in His external glory. The external glory of Mass is CHRIST'S ELECT.

God's MERCY TO HIS ELECT is manifested--and not perceived by most of us--at each Mass. We come to Mass to praise God through Christ; and more specifically, through the Christ-priest who alone celebrates or brings about the Mass-- THE Prayer of Christ to God.

How much should we respect priests! They are like the Holy Ghost. They and they alone can bring Christ's Saving Action and Christ Himself to us in "our" space and time.

Thank God for His priests. Pray for them. Encourage them. Do all you can to assure your children of validly ordained priests and valid Masses.

"It is possible for you to gain more favor with God
by attending or celebrating one single Mass,
considered in itself and in its intrinsic worth,

than by opening the treasury of your wealth
and distributing the whole to the poor, or
by going as a pilgrim over the whole world..."

St. Leonard of Port Maurice

CHAPTER FOURTEEN

EACH MASS--YOUR ONLY SALVATION

"God began whatever began. He began the heavens and the earth (Gn 1:1). Waste, void and cursed (Gn 1:2A). The Holy Ghost, God, ACTED (Gn 1:2B). God the Father and God the Son SPOKE: 'Light be.' Light was (Gn 1:3). Light was good [and darkness was evil] (Gn 1:4A). Light and darkness were separated (Gn 1:4B)."

As any good author, God summarizes His whole Bible in its first paragraph. Here is everything. Here are you--in time and THUS into eternity. Let's see what the Bible tells us in its first four verses (according to my own faith-filled and accurate version).

God is in charge. ELOHIM means "the two or more GOD," and thereby implies the Trinity [in subsequent verses as acting (or breathing) and as speaking take place]. Also the Bible tells us, God is AHAD--absolutely ONE (e.g. Dt 6:4).

God the Father created initially and then RE-PARS (restores the sin-cursed MESS to His ideal or par) through the Son SPEAKING and the Holy Ghost ACTING or BREATHING upon the wasted cursed void or "the Mess."

How did the cursed and emptied waste come about? By SIN or by disobedience to God. Only SIN destroys. This side of death, SIN is the only EVIL since it offends God; and, since it alone can bring YOU into eternal Hell.

Naturally, as children of disobedient Adam through Eve, we are born in; and, usually ratify SIN. Naturally, we are estranged by SIN from God and from dwelling with God in Heaven. Naturally, we are part of THE MESS.

Only the ACTING and SPEAKING of God can change our natural dark FATE into light. ONLY your individual graced choosing to embrace and be part of God's special ACTING and SPEAKING, or to be part of the Saving Light can save you from your natural fate of union with THE mess-cursed darkness, for all eternity.

For all eternity, evil and cursed darkness will be separated from God-blessed and God-endowed LIGHT. According to God's Bible and the testimony of classical saints, FEW (very few) find the narrow door; and then, walk the narrow path which alone can save them from their natural fate.

Few properly respond to God's ACTING AND SPEAKING light or salvation TO DESTROY darkness or damnation. Where, you may ask, IS this ACTING AND SPEAKING?

"God spoke and God speaking" is the WORD--the Second Person of the Trinity (Jn 1:1). Without this Word, nothing is made (Jn 1:3). God the Father "makes anything to be" only through the Son of God (in the power or action of the Holy Ghost).

Salvation is the RE-CREATION. It is the other "making by God." As such, it must be done with or through the Son of God or the Word.

Indeed, this happened and happens. The Word, the Son of God, became flesh (Jn 1:14). Jesus saved. Jesus saves.

The ACTION of salvation is accomplished by the Holy Ghost (Gn 1:2B). The SPEAKING or doing of Salvation is accomplished by the Word of the Father or by God the Father through the Son of God (Gn 1:3; Jn. 1:3). NOTHING comes to BE without the Word (Jn 1:3). Salvation comes to be BY THE WORD.

Remember God's specially chosen "action words"-- ACTING and SPEAKING. These are His words. These bring about and manifest any "making" by God; and ESPECIALLY, God's making salvation or God's selectively recreating or remaking PARTS OF the cursed and emptied darkness into blessed light.

In the end and for all eternity without end LIGHT will be separated from DARKNESS. How? By God's special salutary acting and speaking.

WHERE is such salutary acting and speaking? In every properly celebrated Mass of the Canonized Liturgy.

"Qui pridie quam pateretur accepit panem in sanctas ac venerabiles manus suas, et elevatis oculis in caelum ad te Deum Patrem suum omnipotentem, tibi gratias AGENS bene dixit, fregit, deditque discipulis suis, DICENS:

Accipite, et manducate ex hoc omnes: 'Hoc est enim Corpus Meum.'"

"Who, the day before He suffered, took bread into His Holy and venerable hands, and having lifted up His eyes to heaven, to Thee, God, His Almighty Father, giving thanks to Thee, blessed it, broke it, and gave it to His disciples, saying:

'Take and eat ye all of this, for this is My Body.'"

"Simili modo postquam coenatum est, accipiens et hunc praeclarum Calicem in sanctas, ac venerabiles manus suas: item tibi gratias AGENS, bene dixit, deditque discipulis suis, DICENS:

Accipite, et bibite ex eo omnes, 'Hic est enim calix Sanguinis Mei, novi et aeterni testamenti: Mysterium Fidei: qui pro multis effundetur in remissionem peccatorum.'"

"In like manner, after He had supped, taking also into His holy and venerable hands this precious chalice, again giving thanks to Thee, He blessed it and gave it to His disciples saying:

'Take and drink ye all of this: For this is the Chalice of My Blood, of the new and everlasting testament: the Mystery of Faith: which shall be shed for you and for many unto the remission of sins.'"

"AGENS and DICENS"-- HERE is God's salutary ACTING and SPEAKING. HERE is salvation FROM your "naturally inevitable" communion with eternal MESS.

Without Him--the Word of God, or the Second Person of the Trinity--NOTHING COMES INTO BEING. Therefore, for "THE GREATEST"--THE INFINITELY POSITIVE SIDE OF SALVATION--to come into being, HE must be ACTING (AGENS), with the Father and the Holy Ghost; He must be SAYING (DICENS).

Each validly ordained priest validly consecrates and brings into being the EFFECTIVE SAVING DEED OF CHRIST (the unbloody Sacrifice of Calvary) ONLY by ACTING (AGENS) and SPEAKING (DICENS) in the Person of Christ (in persona Christi).

At the Canonized Mass, Christ ACTS and SPEAKS as THE PRIEST ACTS and SPEAKS. The "Greatest" is being made possible for "GOD'S ELECT" (and no others).

This can ONLY be made and "eternally be" with or through CHRIST (Jn 1:3). Why? "Without HIM, nothing comes to be (Jn 1:3)."

At every valid Mass by a validly ordained priest, YOU are privileged to be at THE GREATEST MAKING. Here is THE SAVING-ACT out of which and within which is THE SAVING-PERSON.

CHRIST again is made flesh. CHRIST again is made blood. CHRIST again is sacrificed.

Calvary is taken out of its own space and time and made present to YOU through the CHRIST-PRIEST in as much as

GOD can do this. Here in a particular space and time Calvary is made present. For all eternity, "Calvary and the Lamb" are the center, source, sustenance and summit of Heaven--"The Lamb once slain" (Re 5:12).

At a valid Mass, YOU are privileged to be at Calvary--Past; at Calvary--Present; and at Calvary--Eternal. Pray; pray; pray that you may be graced to comprehend and always remember what happens at every Canonized Mass.

"Go, show yourselves as my beloved children:

I am with you and in you, provided that your faith
be the light that enlightens you in these days of woe.

May your zeal cause you to be as famished
for the glory and honor of Jesus Christ.

Fight, children of light,
you LITTLE NUMBER WHO SEE CLEARLY.

For behold, the time of times,
the end of ends."

The Secret of La Salette
The Blessed Virgin to Melanie

CHAPTER FIFTEEN

YOUR CHALLENGE

Gracefully cooperate with God's gifts of understanding and wisdom so as to "perceive and perform" your challenge. Your challenge is by God's grace, to participate in THE SAVING-MYSTERY.

You must come to live, not you but Christ in YOU (Ga 2:20). As it were, Christ ACTING (through the Holy Ghost) and SPEAKING (with God the Father) must totally transform BOTH the Bread and Wine; and, your flesh and spirit into Him. That's the open-ended challenge of the Mass for YOU.

As a layman, YOU do not offer Mass. However, YOU can and "must" offer "the chalice of salvation" or "the oblation" in the way described above.

Your honor is to be transformed by Christ's renewing or totally changing your mind from within (Ro 12:2). Thus, you can make up in your body what is lacking of Christ's sufferings in your body for the sake of His Body, the Church (Col 1:24, as in the original Greek).

Therefore, at each Mass, welcome Christ to "ACT and SPEAK Himself" into YOU. Thank Christ. Thank Him by letting Him act and speak THROUGH and IN you.

Strive to live, not you, but Christ in you. Whenever Christ lives in anyone this side of death He lives ONLY to be crucified--to die to the flesh and this world in obedience to the Father's Will. Therefore, live so as to always be dying to your flesh and this world. How? Through, in and with Christ Who is to be or to become your Only Life.

This is LIVING THE MASS. Thus, the ACTING and SPEAKING affects and "effects" YOU.

SUCH is your ONLY escape from the "cursed waste and void." Here, by God's freely given grace, is LIFE.

"God began whatever began. He began the heavens and the earth (Gn 1:1). Waste, void and cursed (Gn 1:2A). The Holy Ghost, God ACTED (Gn 1:2B). God the Father and God the Son SPOKE: 'Light be.' Light was (Gn 1:3). Light was good [and darkness was evil] (Gn 1:4A). Light and darkness were separated" (Gn 1:4B).

Will you naturally be part of the darkness separated from Light? Will you, by God's grace and your graced cooperation, be united to Light for all eternity?

The road to the latter is Crucifixion--the Saving-Act of the Mass. Pray the Holy Mass. Live the Holy Mass.

"A day will come when the civilized world
will deny its God,
WHEN THE CHURCH WILL DOUBT, as Peter doubted.

She will be tempted to believe
THAT MAN HAS BECOME GOD...

IN OUR CHURCHES CHRISTIANS WILL SEARCH IN
VAIN
FOR THE RED LAMP WHERE GOD AWAITS THEM,

like Magdalen weeping before the EMPTY TOMB,
they will ask

'WHERE HAVE THEY TAKEN HIM?'"--Pope Pius XII.

Msgr. Roche
"Pie XII devant l'histoire"
pp. 52-53, caps added.

"...Specifically, do we warn all persons in authority
of whatever dignity or rank, and command them
as a matter of strict obedience
never to use or permit any ceremonies of Mass prayers
other than the ones contained in this Missal...

At no time in the future can a priest,
whether secular or order priest,
ever be forced to use any other way of saying Mass.

And in order once and for all to preclude
any scruples of conscience and
fear of ecclesiastical penalties and censures,
we declare herewith that it is by virtue
of our Apostolic authority
that we decree and prescribe
that this present order and decree of ours
is to last in PERPETUITY,
and never at a future date
can it be revoked or amended legally...

And if, nevertheless, anyone would dare attempt
any action contrary to this order of ours,
handed down for all times,
let him know that he has incurred the wrath
of Almighty God, and of
the Blessed Apostles Peter and Paul."

Pope St. Pius V
QUO PRIMUM

PRAYER FOR THE RETURN OF THE
ROMAN RITE MASS AND LITURGY

O GOD, WHO didst choose Blessed Pius
as supreme Pontiff

in order to shatter the enemies of Thy Church
and to restore the purity of the Sacred Liturgy,

grant us his protection so that,
cleaving to Thy service

we may overcome the snares of all our enemies
and enjoy perpetual peace.

Through Christ Our Lord.
Amen.

From the Mass of St. Pius V
May 5

ST. PIUS V, PRAY FOR US!

MAY THAT LITURGY
WHICH YOU MOST DOGMATICALLY DECREED
AS BEING THE CHURCH'S CANON
ONCE AGAIN BE THE CHURCH'S CANON!

OTHER BOOKS BY FR. TRINCHARD

ALL ABOUT SALVATION

APOSTASY WITHIN

GOD'S WORD

NEW AGE NEW MASS

THE AWESOME FATIMA CONSECRATIONS

NEW MASS IN LIGHT OF THE OLD

DISTRIBUTED BY

CATHOLIC TREASURES
PO BOX 5034
MONROVIA CA 91017-1734